STOCK ANSWERS

STOCK ANSWERS

A Guide to the International Equities Market

Edited by Jonathan Clements

Nichols Publishing
New York

Nichols Publishing Company
PO Box 96, New York, New York 10024 and
155 West 72nd Street, New York, New York 10023.

© Cassell Publishers Limited 1988

First published in 1988 in the United States of America by
Nichols Publishing, an imprint of GP Publishing Inc.
First published in 1988 in Great Britain by
Cassell Publishers Limited
Artillery House, Artillery Row, London SW1P 1RT.

Library of Congress Cataloging in Publication Data
Stock Answers: a guide to the international equities
market/edited by Jonathan Clements.

p.   cm.
Includes index.
ISBN 0–89397–313–0.
1. Investments, Foreign. 2. Stocks.   i. Clements, Jonathan.
HG 4538.S748   1988
332.6'5 – – dc19   88–9906.

Printed and bound in Great Britain at The Bath Press, Avon

Contents

Acknowledgements

The editor and publisher would like to thank the following organizations for their help in preparing this book:

The Black & Decker Corp.
Cleary, Gottlieb, Steen & Hamilton
Credit Suisse First Boston Ltd
Dominion Securities, Inc.
Hanan Associates AG
International Securities Clearing Corp.
Maxicare Health Plans, Inc.
Milbank, Tweed, Hadley & McCloy
Morgan Grenfell (Asia) Ltd
National Association of Securities Dealers, Inc.
Salomon Brothers, Inc.
J. Henry Schroder Wagg & Co. Ltd
Yamaichi International (Europe) Ltd

Notes on the Contributors

Mary Ann Callahan is a vice-president at the International Securities Clearing Corporation, with senior responsibility for ISCC's market development strategy/business planning. Her credentials include 13 years of experience in operational aspects of the financial services industry. Callahan has nearly eight years of settlements experience at the National Securities Clearing Corporation, the parent company of ISCC, where she previously served as vice-president, corporate communications. She holds a BA degree in English literature from Manhattanville College, Purchase, New York, and an MBA in finance from New York University. The opinions expressed in her chapter are not necessarily those of the International Securities Clearing Corporation.

Jonathan Clements was born in London and brought up in the United States and Bangladesh, and is a reporter with *Forbes* magazine in New York. A graduate of Emmanuel College, Cambridge University, he has written for newspapers and magazines in the United States and Britain, including *Euromoney* magazine and the *Independent* of London.

Mitchell S. Dupler, a cum laude graduate of Harvard College and Harvard Law School, is an associate with the Washington office of Cleary, Gottlieb, Steen & Hamilton. From 1982 to 1984, he was an associate in the firm's London office. In both London and Washington, he has been involved in a wide variety of international and US securities transactions.

Thomas Fairhead joined Credit Suisse First Boston Ltd in 1980. Since 1981 he has been active in all aspects of international corporate finance, in particular equity and equity-linked issues and foreign stock exchange listings. He has written for, among other publications, *The Treasurer* magazine.

Jerome L. Hanan, chairman of Hanan Associates AG in Zurich, Switzerland, was born in Long Island, New York, and studied at Ohio State University, the Sorbonne and the University of Heidelberg. His international assignments include work for the US Government in Germany, followed by executive positions as director of Corporate Affairs, Europe and the Middle East, for Litton Industries in Paris and vice-president and managing director of City Investing Company's European office in Zurich. Hanan Associates AG was established in 1979 and now has affiliate offices in London, Paris, Dusseldorf and Tokyo.

Larry A. Kimmel is a vice-president and compliance manager for Salomon Brothers, Inc. Recently he was domiciled in Salomon's London office to establish a Compliance Department which oversees its European sales and trading efforts. Prior to joining Salomon Brothers, Inc. Kimmel was the national coordinator for the National Association of Securities Dealers Clearing Corporation. He graduated cum laude from Pace University in 1976 with a Masters Degree (MBA) in finance. Kimmel received his Bachelors of Business Administration (BBA) from the City College of New York in 1969.

Richard Lazarus is an assistant director in the Corporate Finance Department of Schroders, principally involved in the execution of new issues. Prior to joining Schroders in 1983, he spent ten years with the merchant bank N. M. Rothschild & Sons Ltd, which he joined after leaving Cambridge. He is a fellow of the Chartered Association of Certified Accountants.

Cheryl I. Leonhardt joined Dominion Securities, Inc. in July 1986 as part of the firm's newly established generalist programme which, over a two-year period, will give her the opportunity to work in almost all professional areas of the firm. She has completed a term in institutional equity trading, specifically trading research and theoretical and real arbitrage trading, and is presently working with the firm's mergers and acquisitions group. Prior to joining DS, she completed an honours degree in business administration at the University of Western Ontario. Her thanks to Gary Selke and Rod Macgillivray, both of Dominion Securities, Inc. for their insight into the Canadian bought deal market.

Albert F. Lilley, a graduate of Bowdoin College and the University of Virginia Law School, is a partner with Milbank, Tweed, Hadley & McCloy in New York, specializing in public and private finance with an emphasis upon representing foreign private issuers, foreign governments and their agencies in connection with financing in the US capital markets. He is a member of the American Bar Association, the New York State Bar Association, the Association of the Bar of the City of New York and the American Law Institute.

Gordon S. Macklin was president of the National Association of Securities Dealers, Inc. for 17 years before becoming chairman and co-chief executive of Hambrecht & Quist, a San Francisco-based investment bank, in July 1987. An economics graduate of Brown University, Macklin joined McDonald & Co., a regional securities firm in Cleveland, Ohio, as a trainee in 1950. In 1951, he founded an office for the company in Findlay, Ohio, before returning to Cleveland in 1958 as a partner in the sales management and syndicate department. From 1962 to 1970, he was in the company's corporate finance department and a member of the firm's executive committee. He has served on the board of governors of the NASD and the Midwest Stock Exchange, as well as on the board of directors of numerous corporations.

John O'Donnell is a graduate of the National University of Ireland (UCC) where he completed a B.Comm, B.C.L., LL.B. He was also called to the Irish Bar. On completing his education, he joined Yamaichi International (Europe) Limited, the UK operation of Yamaichi Securities, one of the Big Four Japanese investment banks. Having pioneered their syndicate activities, he is now involved in developing their mergers and acquisitions capability in Europe, building on Yamaichi's leading position in this area in Japan.

Stephen F. Page is vice-president for finance and treasurer of the Black & Decker Corporation and is responsible for treasury, tax, accounting and control functions. He was appointed treasurer in April 1982 and assumed additional responsibility for finance in December 1985. Page was formerly employed as vice-president, secretary and general counsel of McCulloch Corporation of Los Angeles, and joined Black & Decker when it acquired McCulloch as a subsidiary in 1972. After serving in various legal and financial positions, he was appointed chief financial officer of Black & Decker's Americas International Group in 1981. This group comprised operating units in North and South America, Australia and the Far East. Page is a graduate of Loyola University, Los Angeles, California, where he received a BBA degree in accounting. He also holds a JD degree from the Loyola University Law School.

Quek Peck Lim is head of research at Morgan Grenfell (Asia) Securities in Singapore. For over four years he was an assistant editor at *Euromoney* magazine in London, specializing in international equity issues. He conceived and helped edit a guide to the world's stock markets, published by Euromoney Publications.

Robert Swannell, after qualifying as a chartered accountant with Peat, Marwick, Mitchell in 1973, trained to become a barrister and was called to the Bar in 1976, thereafter specializing in company law and taxation. He joined the Corporate Finance Division of J. Henry Schroder Wagg & Co. Ltd in 1977. He was appointed a director in 1985 and at that time was responsible for Schroders' new issues activities in the UK.

Dr Fred W. Wasserman is chairman and chief executive officer of Los Angeles-based Maxicare Health Plans, Inc., America's largest publicly-traded health maintenance organization. With his wife, Pamela K. Anderson, and a group of physicians he founded Maxicare as a small community health plan in 1972 with $37 000. Today, the company serves 2.3 million members in 26 states and operates in more major markets than any other HMO company. In demand as a public speaker because of his expertise in managed health care, Dr Wasserman also continues to teach at both the University of California at Los Angeles (UCLA) and the University of Southern California (USC), and is widely published in professional journals.

For Clem

Chapter 1

Introduction

Even Libya's Colonel Qaddafi uses the international equity market. In 1986, the country was suffering from the fall in world oil prices, which had cut the flow of much-needed foreign currency. Economic sanctions by the United States and some European countries further exacerbated Libya's problems. The Colonel needed money. An unwilling business associate of the Libyan government had trouble of his own. The Italian car manufacturer Fiat SpA, headed by Giovanni Agnelli, was beginning to suffer from the notoriety caused by Libya's share-holding in the company. A decade earlier, the Libyan government had purchased a 15.19% stake in Fiat when the company was battling against labour trouble and losses. By 1986, however, the company was prospering – except, however, when it came to contracts from the US government, including a share of the work on Reagan's Strategic Defense Initiative. Following international outrage at alleged Libyan sponsorship of world terrorism, which led to America's retaliatory bombing of Libya, the US government balked at the idea of doing business with Fiat, fearing that the resulting profits would only finance the terrorism it was fighting against.

Agnelli sought to buy out the Libyans. The Libyans said no. Then something changed. Possibly Libya's foreign currency situation deteriorated. Possibly the stock market suddenly seemed brighter. Whatever the reason, the Libyans decided to deal. Secret negotiations began in Zurich. A price was found. Libya was to receive $3.15 billion, almost eight times more than its initial $400 million investment. It was the type of capital gain most portfolio managers would be proud of. The Colonel not only got his money, he also got the last laugh. What emerged from the negotiations was the largest Euro-equity offering ever. It was also one of the most complex and troublesome.

The deal, launched in late September 1986, was structured in three parts. The Agnelli family took shares worth $1.05 billion, raising their stake in Fiat to 41%. The remaining securities, a mixture of preference shares, common stock and savings shares worth $2.1 billion, were divided between an Italian and an international syndicate. The Italian syndicate, a group of nine co-managers led by Mediobanca, placed securities worth $500 million. That left the Deutsche

1

Bank-led syndicate to place $1.6 billion of Fiat securities in the international market. It all went wrong.

The deal may have been doomed by its very size. But the problems that emerged, whatever their cause, serve to highlight the difficulties now being encountered as the nascent international equity market seeks to imitate the already global bond market. Possibly the effort to imitate is in itself part of the problem. The international trading of US treasury bonds, and the emergence of the Eurobond placement market, has provided equity market participants with a powerful – if not always beneficial – example. Put simply, bonds are not equities and any attempt to treat the two instruments in the same fashion can be disastrous. Bonds may be sold on coupon and issue price (among other attributes), but equities are sold on fundamentals; earnings, expectations, past performance. Selling equities is also more sensitive. When a bond issue goes badly, the lead manager's reputation is hurt and the corporate issuer has a certain smug satisfaction that it raised money cheaply. But with an equity issue, a company's reputation in the market dives if its stock price starts to tumble. With the Fiat issue, confusion over settlement procedures and uncoordinated selling encouraged international investors and some of the issue's management group to sell the stock back into the home market. The price of Fiat dropped on the Milan stock exchange, further undercutting the issue's credibility. Some houses used bond salesmen to sell equities, a usually safe tactic in a rising market when investors are less discerning about the stocks they buy. When share prices are falling, however, investors need to be persuaded of a stock's true worth, and that demands good, fundamental research and salesmen well-versed about the issue. Without expert selling and good coordination of the syndicate by the lead manager, an issue can quickly fall apart, with investors receiving innumerable calls from different salesmen, all offering the same stock at widely differing prices. While the Fiat issue will not be remembered as a wildly successful issue, the syndicate did work to pull together the issue, partly compensating for the initial rout. Deutsche Bank reportedly bought back a substantial amount of stock, creating pockets of demand and lifting market confidence. Whatever losses were incurred by the banks involved, they were undoubtedly less than they could have been.

The Fiat issue, in addition to highlighting the problems of international equity issues, also rekindled the debate about the best method for placing stock abroad. So-called Euro-equity issues, in which a separate syndicate is used to place shares outside the home market, have become increasingly popular since 1983. These issues attract attention in the press and earn abundant kudos for the investment banks concerned. But Euro-equity syndicates are just one of many methods for placing shares abroad, and these syndicates are not always the most appropriate. Since the early 1960s, Japanese companies have used depository receipts to issue equity internationally. Deals involving convertible bonds and bonds with warrants continue to account for much of the new issue volume. Combined or domestic-only syndicates, where a single group of banks place stock both at home and abroad, have been used for many years by US investment banks. Cross-border block placements, often unpublicized, have the longest pedigree of all, dating back to the nineteenth century when they were used to finance railway construction in Asia and the Americas.

While this array of issuing methods serves to ridicule the notion that Euro-equity syndicates are the most important segment of the market, nonetheless the emergence of the Euro-equity market has had a significance greater than its size. In these deals, corporate treasurers have made a conscious decision that they want 10% or 25% or 50% of a stock issue placed with international investors. With other methods, such as convertible bonds or combined syndicates, the international placement of equity sometimes seems a secondary consideration, something that resulted because demand was poor in the home market or because the equity was a sweetener for an otherwise unattractive bond issue. Moreover, Euro-equity syndicates were given added credibility when major privatizations such as KLM, Britoil and British Telecom employed this issuing technique.

Developments in the international issuing of equity are only part of the story. Structural impediments to international stock trading are now starting to crumble. The signs of internationalization are everywhere. In late 1986, the Stock Exchange in London renamed itself the International Stock Exchange. The National Securities Clearing Corporation set up a new subsidiary, the International Securities Clearing Corporation, in 1985. Exchanges are establishing links with each other, Boston with Montreal, Toronto with the American Stock Exchange, London with the National Association of Securities Dealers. Similar developments are now taking place among the options and futures exchanges. In the pages that follow, these and other developments are discussed and analysed.

In Chapter 2, for instance, Jonathan Clements and Quek Peck Lim look at how equity is placed abroad through syndicates and block placements. The emergence of Euro-equity offerings may be symbolic of the global market's development, but these straight equity issues have also been controversial, with questions raised about the appropriate method of syndication and the problem of flowback of equity to the domestic market in the aftermath of an international stock offering. Moreover, these syndicated equity issues are not the only way to place equity abroad, nor are they the most complex. A stock is a stock. Or is it? Investment bankers are adopting increasingly creative solutions as they try to offload large blocks of shares. How do you sell shares worth $50 million or $100 million without depressing the stock's price? Look abroad, using bonds, notes, warrants and all the banking wisdom you can muster. Thomas Fairhead elaborates on the subject of warrants and convertible bonds in Chapter 3. These hybrid securities have proved the most popular instruments for placing equity with eager international investors, especially those fund managers prohibited from making straight equity investments. Such offerings can also help corporate issuers meet a number of objectives by, for example, improving the company's balance sheet while at the same time placing stock beyond the reach of corporate raiders.

In Chapter 4, Larry Kimmel describes the operation and effect of Rule 415. In Chapter 5, Cheryl Leonhardt describes the new, high risk game that has emerged as a result of the Canadian bought deal. The two chapters explain how banks in Canada and the US can – within days if not hours – bring a deal to the market, grabbing market opportunities as soon as they occur. Both chapters describe the growing concentration of deals in the hands of fewer and fewer investment banks. With that concentration comes growing rewards for the banks that can compete. But with those rewards also come risks, and not just from sudden, adverse market movements. Under great time pressure to get issues to market, banks are now running the legal risk that the corporate prospectuses they circulate and the registration statements that they file may contain misstatements or omissions. The lessons learned from Canada and the United States could prove valuable to those contemplating the bought deal's use in the international market. While the bought bond deal is now commonplace in the Euromarkets, the bought equity deal has to date been seen as too risky.

Stephen Page, Black & Decker's treasurer, writes about the company's experience of the international equity market. Confronted by a faltering stock market and a fickle investment community, the company managed to tap both the European and the North American markets simultaneously. For a company that had just restructured itself, this was an astonishing achievement. The story is told in Chapter 14. The 1985 international equity offering by Maxicare Health Plans, Inc. was also remarkable, though for different reasons. The company's Euro-equity issue was, more than anything else, a triumph of international investor relations. Unlike Black & Decker, Maxicare does not sell its product abroad. Nonetheless, through a gradual cultivation of foreign investors, the company ensured strong investor interest for its international offering. This process of cultivation is described by Fred Wasserman, the company's chairman, in Chapter 15.

As Maxicare's example shows, the international offering of equity is more than just a two-day selling operation. The smiling and dialling by equity salesmen is often the culmination of months of market preparation. As Jerome Hanan tells in Chapter 11, international investor relations has emerged as an important tool for any company wanting to expand or issue securities abroad. And the job isn't over when the final share is sold. To maintain shareholder loyalty – and prevent the flowback of stock to the home market – involves an ongoing programme of regular advertising, meetings with investors and distribution of information about the company.

The cost of participating in a market is measured in more than just trading commissions and gross underwriting spreads. National market regulation is a key determinant in the development of markets, as evidenced by the emergence of the Eurodollar market beyond the taxing hand of Congress and the regulatory grasp of the US Securities and Exchange Commission (SEC). For foreign corporations, the US capital market has long seemed an almost impregnable fortress; the goodies on offer within the walls may be tempting, but the cost of getting there isn't. In Chapter 8, Albert Lilley guides readers through the array of US regulations. As he mentions, the SEC has already made some concessions to foreign issuers wanting to tap the US market. And, as Mitchell Dupler explains in Chapter 9, further changes are in the offing. The SEC has issued a discussion document that may eventually lead the US, UK and Canada to adopt a common or reciprocal prospectus for both international debt and equity securities issues.

With US regulation seeming so excessive, many corporations have avoided the market, including US companies themselves. In Chapter 6, Robert Swannell and Richard Lazarus describe the welcome received by US companies going public in London, noting that there are 'suspicions that foreign companies come to London following an unsuccessful effort to persuade their compatriots of their virtues'. But, as the chapter describes, these suspicions can be overcome with careful preparation and skilful execution.

Japanese issuers, too, have fought shy of the US market, preferring to tap the Euromarkets when seeking foreign capital. In Chapter 7, John O'Donnell guides readers through the Japanese capital markets, explaining why the shares of Japanese companies are not overpriced but why, at the same time, the thirst for foreign equity is increasing among Japan's investors. With Japan's cash surplus mounting, no internationally-oriented corporation can afford to ignore the country's investors.

The development of clearing and settlement services has emerged as a key dynamic in the growth of a global equity market. A foreign stock may look like a good investment but the attractive price/earnings ratio could be swallowed up by cumbersome and costly clearing. 'There is an ever-increasing risk that trading profits may become administrative losses', writes Mary Ann Callahan in Chapter 10. Similar problems have dogged the growth of the global options and futures market. Though the exchanges have introduced innumerable different contracts, it seems less effort has been put into international clearing. As outlined in Chapter 13, the global market in derivative instruments has enjoyed much experimentation but little trading volume. It is still uncertain how the market will develop.

No such doubts are expressed in Chapter 12. Gordon Macklin, president of the National Association of Securities Dealers (NASD) for 17 years, describes how he thinks the 24-hour market will develop. One of the most vigorous proponents both of the electronic marketplace and of the competitive multiple market maker system, Mr Macklin looks at the recent link between the NASD and the London Stock Exchange. If London's Big Bang is viewed as an argument, then Gordon Macklin is on the winning side. Offered a choice between the trading floor and the computer terminal, London's traders chose to stay in their offices.

While the views expressed in each chapter are not necessarily endorsed by other contributors, nonetheless this book will hopefully provide readers with a comprehensive view of the emerging international equity market. With a book involving so many authors, there are also many to thank. All the contributors showed great patience with the editor, continuing to talk to him despite his pestering phone calls and unreasonable demands. Paul Chinchar and Laura Jereski kindly read and constructively commented on various chapters. George Bull's help and advice was invaluable, taking me under his wing and providing encouragement just when I thought all was going wrong. At Cassell, Simon Lake helped get the book under way and Diana Russell saw it through to fruition. Both displayed admirable sound judgment and diligence. Most of the abundant paranoia associated with this book was suffered by Molly, who would talk to me over dinner about her day and then realize I wasn't listening. The accusation would come swift and decisive: 'It's the book again, isn't it?' Finally, this book is dedicated to my grandfather, Clem, who has a lean and hungry look and thinks too much.

Jonathan Clements
Princeton, New Jersey
December 1987

Chapter 2

Syndicated Equities, Block Deals and Private Placements

Jonathan Clements and Quek Peck Lim

In a mood reminiscent of the Eurobond market almost two decades ago, companies have used Euro-equity offerings to tap the international equity capital markets in unprecedented numbers during 1986–87. But this activity is also reminiscent of earlier centuries when block placements of equity were used to finance railroads, mines and plantations in North and South America and in the Far East. Since organized stock exchanges began proliferating throughout the world in this century, the trading of equity across borders has accelerated. The primary and secondary markets have become truly global.

The principal methods by which companies have tapped the international capital markets are through sales of new equity to international investors using the overseas branches of domestic underwriters (domestic-only syndicates) and, a more recent development, through a dual-tranche offering, otherwise known as a Euro-equity issue. In addition, companies, as well as large shareholders, have tapped international investors through the block placement of existing shares, whereby an investment bank has traditionally acted as an agent on a 'best efforts' basis. But the nature of the block placement market is changing, and it is starting increasingly to resemble the market for syndicated equities. This chapter looks at both the block placement market and the dual-tranche concept of syndication.

DUAL-TRANCHE OFFERINGS

The development of the international market for dual-tranche primary issues and initial public offerings has been primarily demand-driven, assisted by the bull market of 1982–87 and the increased investor awareness of cross-border opportunities. This increased awareness is, in part, due to the publicity surrounding the privatization programmes in the United Kingdom, France and Canada, the improvement in information flows and the deregulation of certain markets. All told these factors have created an environment favourable

Table 2.1: *Common stock offerings with dual US/Euro-tranche structures 1 Jan. 1985–31 Mar. 1987*

US issue date	Company	Dollar amount of US tranche ($ millions)	Dollar amount of European tranche ($ millions)	Total amount raised ($ millions)	Total shares in US tranche*	Total shares in European tranche*	Total shares offered*	Offer price	European lead manager†
18/7/85	Student Loan Marketing Association	107.0	51.7	158.7	3 100 000	1 500 000	4 600 000	34.50	CSFB
25/9/85	Pacific Telesis Group	353.1	70.6	423.7	5 000 000	1 000 000	6 000 000	70.625	CSFB
26/11/85	Maxicare Health Plans Inc.	90.6	18.1	108.7	5 000 000	1 000 000	6 000 000	18.125	SALI
15/1/86	The Black & Decker Corporation	130.8	40.3	171.1	6 500 000	2 000 000	8 500 000	20.125	SALI
7/2/86	Transamerica Corporation	155.1	38.8	193.9	4 400 000	1 100 000	5 500 000	35.25	SBCI
25/2/86	Chesebrough Pond's Inc.	202.5	40.5	243.0	5 000 000	1 000 000	6 000 000	40.50	SLBI
21/3/86	Morgan Stanley Group Inc.	163.9	90.4	254.3	2 900 000	1 600 000	4 500 000	56.50	MSI
26/3/86	KLM Royal Dutch Airlines	140.4	167.1	307.5	6 850 000	8 150 000	15 000 000	20.50	MLI
10/4/86	H. F. Ahmanson & Company	190.1	63.4	253.5	3 000 000	1 000 000	4 000 000	63.375	MLI
14/4/86	Conagra, Inc.	196.8	48.0	244.8	4 100 000	1 000 000	5 100 000	48.00	MSI
6/5/86	The Bear Stearns Companies Inc.	108.5	52.5	161.0	3 100 000	1 500 000	4 600 000	35.00	SBCI
9/5/86	Fireman's Fund Corporation	265.6	66.4	332.0	6 400 000	1 600 000	8 000 000	41.50	SLBI
14/5/86	The Travelers Corporation	246.3	49.2	295.5	5 000 000	1 000 000	6 000 000	49.25	MSI
20/5/86	The Henley Group Inc.	1190.0	85.0	1275.0	56 000 000	4 000 000	60 000 000	21.25	CSFB
21/5/86	The Prospect Group, Inc.	73.1	24.4	97.5	7 500 000	2 500 000	10 000 000	9.75	SLBI
18/6/86	Trenwick	62.1	13.8	75.9	2 700 000	600 000	3 300 000	23.00	MSI
18/6/86	Citicorp	232.5	58.1	290.6	4 000 000	1 000 000	5 000 000	58.125	SALI
25/6/86	Harcourt Brace Jovanovich, Inc.	108.6	33.0	141.6	3 290 000	1 000 000	4 290 000	33.00	CSFB
9/7/86	Bernard Chaus Inc.	76.5	25.5	102.0	4 500 000	1 500 000	6 000 000	17.00	MLI
1/8/86	Leslie Fay Companies, Inc.	72.0	22.5	94.5	4 000 000	1 250 000	5 250 000	18.00	MLI
12/8/86	American Television & Communications Corp.	268.3	64.7	333.0	14 500 000	3 500 000	18 000 000	18.50	CSFB
20/8/86	Consolidated Stores Corporation	70.0	17.5	87.5	4 000 000	1 000 000	5 000 000	17.50	MLI

Source: Shearson Lehman Brothers.

* Total number of shares offered, as stated on front cover of prospectus. If best efforts, the minimum number of shares is included.

† ALEXI, Alex Brown International; CSFB, Credit Suisse First Boston; GSI, Goldman Sachs International; KPI, Kidder Peabody International; MLI, Merrill Lynch International; MSI, Morgan Stanley International; SALI, Salomon Brothers International; SLBI, Shearson Lehman Brothers International; SBCI, Swiss Bank Corporation International.

Table 2.1: *Common stock offerings with dual US/Euro-tranche structures 1 Jan. 1985–31 Mar. 1987*

US issue date	Company	Dollar amount of US tranche ($ millions)	Dollar amount of European tranche ($ millions)	Total amount raised ($ millions)	Total shares in US tranche*	Total shares in European tranche*	Total shares offered*	Offer price	European lead manager†
8/22/86	Biogen	31.3	6.3	37.6	2 500 000	500 000	3 000 000	12.50	CSFB
25/9/86	SCOR U.S. Corp.	43.5	14.5	58.0	3 000 000	1 000 000	4 000 000	14.50	SLBI
3/10/86	Field Crest Cannon	44.5	9.5	54.0	1 400 000	300 000	1 700 000	31.75	KPI
9/10/86	United Airlines	232.0	58.0	290.0	4 000 000	1 000 000	5 000 000	58.0	MSI
16/10/86	Chemical Waste Management	248.4	62.1	310.5	14 400 000	3 600 000	18 000 000	17.25	MLI
29/10/86	Silicon Graphics	16.2	4.1	20.3	1 440 000	360 000	1 800 000	11.25	MSI
29/10/86	Commercial Credit	662.2	116.9	779.1	32 300 000	5 700 000	38 000 000	20.50	CSFB
6/11/86	Hershey Foods Corp.	83.1	23.8	106.9	3 500 000	1 000 000	4 500 000	23.75	GSI
26/11/86	Coca-Cola Enterprises Inc.	1001.4	176.7	1178.1	60 690 000	10 710 000	71 400 000	16.50	CSFB
26/11/86	Aristech Chemical	319.5	79.9	399.4	18 000 000	4 500 000	22 500 000	17.75	SLBI
12/12/86	Union Carbide Corp.	478.1	84.4	562.5	21 250 000	3 750 000	25 000 000	22.50	CSFB
16/12/86	Bank of Boston	84.2	25.3	109.5	2 000 000	600 000	2 600 000	42.125	SALI
16/12/86	Taiwan Fund	21.4	3.0	24.4	1 776 250	253 750	2 030 000	12.00	MLI
17/12/86	Alliant Computer Systems	21.8	4.5	26.3	1 450 000	300 000	1 750 000	15.00	MSI
19/12/86	Navistar, Inc.	429.2	75.7	504.9	90 351 353	15 944 358	106 295 721	4.75	SLBI
16/1/87	Bowater	88.1	35.3	123.4	2 500 000	1 000 000	3 500 000	35.25	CSFB
21/1/87	Western Auto Supply	46.8	11.7	58.5	3 600 000	900 000	4 500 000	13.00	SLBI
23/1/87	Network Equipment	34.0	6.0	40.0	2 125 000	375 000	2 500 000	16.00	MSI
6/2/87	Federal National Mortgage	289.5	96.5	386.0	6 000 000	2 000 000	8 000 000	48.25	CSFB
12/2/87	Himont	287.0	63.0	350.0	10 250 000	2 250 000	12 500 000	28.00	CSFB
24/2/87	Foodmaker	43.2	10.8	54.0	3 200 000	800 000	4 000 000	13.50	MSI
5/3/87	Telematics International	24.6	6.0	30.6	2 050 000	500 000	2 550 000	12.00	ALEXI
26/3/87	Consolidated Rail	1456.0	189.0	1645.0	52 000 000	6 750 000	58 750 000	28.00	GSI
27/3/87	Harnischfeger Industries, Inc.	42.5	17.0	59.5	2 500 000	1 000 000	3 500 000	17.00	SLBI

Source: Shearson Lehman Brothers.

* Total number of shares offered, as stated on front cover of prospectus. If best efforts, the minimum numerum of shares is included.

† ALEXI, Alex Brown International; CSFB, Credit Suisse First Boston; GSI, Goldman Sachs International; KPI, Kidder Peabody International; MLI, Merrill Lynch International; MSI, Morgan Stanley International; SALI, Salomon Brothers International; SLBI, Shearson Lehman Brothers International; SBCI, Swiss Bank Corporation International.

to issuers, as evidenced by the explosive growth in international equity financings.

A dual-tranche offering involves constructing two parallel syndicates, one to deal solely with the domestic market and the other focusing on the international market. Frequently, the lead underwriter of the domestic syndicate will perform the same function in the international offering. The dual-tranche method of syndication addresses the problems associated with both achieving a wide distribution of shares to international investors and also the need to control such distribution. In addition, such syndicates ensure that foreign banks participating in a syndicate are given greater responsibility. Though foreign banks are often invited into domestic-only syndicates, they are often relatively unimportant members who are given minimal amounts of stock. These foreign banks often end up placing their stock in the domestic rather than the foreign market.

During 1983–85, when the dual-tranche market first became established, the issuers were most likely to be Swiss or Canadian or British. But during 1986–87, US companies have become the major users of the dual-tranche market (see Table 2.1). These companies have been drawn to the offshore market by such intangible benefits as the potential to establish an international investor base, create a presence in the non-domestic capital markets and increase their global profile. These issuers were also attracted by very tangible benefits such as the ability to execute a larger transaction and, in the case of an initial public offering (IPO), realize a higher price for the shares. Indeed, many of the recent dual-tranche offerings have been IPOs.

The dual-tranche concept has also proved very popular among international investors, especially when compared to a domestic-only syndicate. Because a specific number of shares are dedicated to the international market, this increases the international investor's chance of receiving shares in the final allotment. But a dual-tranche offering raises a certain number of issues not related to a domestic-only syndicate. Among the issues raised are the problem of the flowback of equity to the domestic market and the debate surrounding the method of syndication, particularly the question of global versus regional syndicates.

The banking syndicate for the international tranche of a dual-tranche issue can be organized either on a global basis or on a regional basis. American lead-managers have tended to favour global syndicates, while the European banks lean towards using regional syndicates. If a syndicate is structured on a global basis, there are no geographical selling restrictions on its members. By contrast, a syndicate organized on a regional basis limits members to placing stock only in designated countries.

Global syndication

In a globally syndicated offering, the lead manager chooses syndicate members on criteria other than geographical situation. The chief considerations which are taken into account when choosing syndicate members are:

- The need to maximize geographical diversification as much as possible without placing any regional selling restrictions on syndicate members.
- The wish to include banks with complementary placing abilities. The syndicate should include both banks with strong marketing abilities among institutional investors and also banks with the capacity to tap a broad range of retail investors.
- The need to identify syndicate members which are capable and willing to maintain interest in, and demand for, the stock in the secondary market. This would include an ability to provide research reports on the company.

It is often argued that a globally syndicated offering, structured with these considerations in mind, offers a company the most effective route for placing shares among investors with genuine demand while at the same time minimizing the risk of equity flowback and thus reducing the chance of price disruption in the period immediately following the offering.

Regional syndication

In a regionally syndicated offering, a bank or a group of banks act as exclusive placing agent(s) of the securities for a designated country or area to which a specific amount of stock is allocated. The main effort of the syndicate members is then concentrated on trying to find demand matching the regional allocation. The regionally syndicated offering has less application for initial public offerings and companies not well known in the international markets. In these instances, it is difficult to assess the level of demand expected in different countries prior to the launch of the issue. It is therefore difficult to ensure that the amount of stock allocated to each country corresponds to actual demand. As a result, flowback can occur. Moreover, critics of the regional syndication method argue that the issue is not placed on the basis of genuine investor interest but rather on the 'muscle' of the various exclusive placing agents. Nonetheless, this method can make controlling a syndicate easier. For instance, it ensures that investors do not get called by different banks offering the same stock at significantly different prices.

FLOWBACK

The development of the international equity market for dual-tranche issues has been hindered by 'flowback' whereby shares placed in the international market return to the home market, often depressing the stock price on the domestic stock exchange. Dramatic flowback to the UK occurred during the British Telecom offering. This partly reflected excess UK demand. But it also happened because US retail investors were not allocated a sufficient amount of stock compared to the sophisticated institutions, which took their profits when the price moved up. The entire US issue of 18.2 million American Depository Receipts (ADRs) turned over in the first 10 days of trading in the US. Subsequently, trading volumes in the US declined significantly.

Flowback is generally caused by differences in stock market strengths, currency values and trading liquidities in a particular stock. In addition, flowback can be exacerbated by the following factors:

- *Pricing*. If the issue price is excessively conservative, this tends to generate tremendous excess demand in the home market.
- *Special attraction for domestic investors*. If the shares offered are part of a domestic stock market index, demand in the home market increases dramatically, particularly among institutional investors whose performance is judged relative to the index.
- *Allocation size*. If the allocation of shares to the international market is small, this prevents an organized placement of the issue taking place among institutional and retail investors. It also reduces liquidity in the international market and induces foreign investors to go to the home market for liquidity.

Buyers of foreign equities, for the most part, tend to be sophisticated financial institutions seeking short-term profits. Confronted by significant price movements in the stock, these investors trade actively and are only prepared to hold shares for a short period of time. They also tend to rely on the home market, thus contributing to the flowback problem. Nonetheless, there are a number of ways to minimize the flowback of equity to the home market. The underwriters can reduce flowback by organizing and supervising the distribution of the shares to a carefully selected mix of retail and institutional investors who are the natural buyers of such equities or of stocks from that particular industry sector. In addition, investor demand can be cultivated and maintained through regular research reports and frequent meetings with management. Well-informed investors are less likely to sell their positions in an abrupt fashion.

Since the beginning of 1986, the dual-tranche has become a major feature of the international equity capital markets. The continued expansion of these offerings depends on many factors, including international investment attitudes towards foreign corporations, the willingness of investors to assume currency risks and the state of the equity markets in general. On the positive side, this method of offering has afforded many companies access to markets which, in the past, they may have considered closed. Among the potential candidates for a dual-tranche issue are: companies with significant international operations looking to match business and investor exposure geographically; companies wishing to establish a major international profile with a view to future financings; and companies in industries which are more highly valued offshore.

BLOCK DEALS AND PRIVATE PLACEMENTS

The growing appetite for equities has spawned a wave of investment banking creativity, with the invention of new equity instruments and equity hybrids to finance or sweeten acquisitions. The net result has been the growing availability of shares for big block placements and the consequent demand on brokers to find secure holders for these stocks and thus avoid depressing the market price. As a consequence, the value and volume of these placements has increased over the years. In the past, block deals above $20 million were a rarity. Now international investors are capable of absorbing $50 to $100 million. The nature of these block placements has also changed. Where before large secondary offerings were sold by brokers on a 'best efforts' basis, today the biggest deals involve a syndicate of banks. Indeed, some recent secondary placements, such as those for Fiat, Daimler Benz and Reuters (described below), have used the Euro-equity style of offering. As such, these issues have had to deal with the same syndication problems as those mentioned above for international IPOs and primary issues.

Like the growth of the dual-tranche syndicate, the growing volume of cross-border equity deals has been fuelled partly through the geographic diversification of portfolios by both institutional investors and high net worth individuals. But the market for the placement of large secondary stock offerings has also been fuelled by the arbitrage opportunities available as a result of multiple stock exchange listings by individual companies. For instance, the shares of AT&T are listed on the New York, London, Zurich, Frankfurt and Amsterdam stock exchanges. Because of the electronic link between the London Stock Exchange's SEAQ system and the US National Association of Securities Dealers' NASDAQ system, AT&T is now also available to NASDAQ dealers as well as New York Stock Exchange members. Multiple listings thus provide arbitrage opportunities not just for foreign investors, but also for different types of investors within the same country.

As corporations around the world developed and matured, their capital requirements gradually outstripped the capacity of their founding owner-managers. The private placement market grew out of an attempt by corporate management and/or major shareholders to sell off large blocks of equity without depressing the stock's market price. It was natural that, in their search for secure shareholders, they would turn abroad for new investors. Original shareholders soon found that by using the international market they were able to raise new capital at a premium. By contrast, in the local market, the issue of new shares by way of a rights issue would have meant selling at a discount to the existing market price. Similarly, large shareholders found that the international market allowed them to sell their own shares in big blocks without depressing the current value of the stock.

Since 1980, the pace of international equity dealings has accelerated even further. From 1985 to 1987, market after market around the world hit successive record highs both in volume and value terms. The worldwide bull market was assisted by an easing of foreign exchange restrictions, investment controls, pension fund rules and market regulations. On-line real time price reporting on a global basis has become a daily reality through the use of electronics. Linkages between stock exchanges across the globe has made round the clock trading in equities possible and profitable. In early 1987 NASDAQ and the Singapore Stock Exchange signed an agreement to exchange prices on a selected group of equities quoted on NASDAQ so that trading in these shares could occur in Singapore during those hours when the US market is closed. The infrastructure for international stock trading is now being laid.

The demand for international equities has also begun to grow. As inflation eased during the 1980s, investors began shifting a growing proportion of their funds out of fixed income bonds and into equity. Pension fund rules have also been amended to allow investment managers to shift a growing portion of their funds into foreign securities. InterSec Research Inc., a US-based company that tracks these investment flows, estimates that ERISA funds (so-called because of the US Employee Retirement Income Security Act of 1974) invested overseas totalled $27 billion in 1985 and predicts the total will run to $120 billion by 1990. The Japanese, with their huge capital surplus, have been slow to diversify abroad. They have less than 1% of their investible funds in foreign equities. But already the growing interest in foreign equities has led to the emergence of a host of specialist money managers concentrating on profitable market niches. There are now managers who concentrate on everything from the volatile Bangkok stock market to growth companies in Scandinavia.

These specialist fund managers have demanded, and received, research that compares companies from different countries but which operate in the same industry. They have brought different investment criteria to these stocks and have in the process re-rated many moribund equities. And because these fund managers understand foreign markets, they have become the target of investment bankers and stockbrokers who are seeking secure investors for large blocks of stock. These investors tend to be stable holders of equity, helping to prevent the flowback of stocks to the domestic market. Their ability to take a long-term view provides the confidence necessary for the market's growth.

RECENT BLOCK PLACEMENTS

In October 1986, for instance, American and British investors were given a chance to participate in the French market when $100 million worth of French blue chip and second line stocks were placed abroad in one of the biggest block placements of its kind. The transaction, amounting to roughly a single day's trading volume on the Paris bourse, appears to have been placed securely with firm holders. There have been few signs of the dreaded flowback of this stock into the French market. The French experience, made all the more memorable by the fact that it was placed overseas by the securities subsidiary of a British merchant bank, is increasingly common. During 1986, at least half-a-dozen Malaysian companies have had large blocks of their shares placed in Singapore, Hong Kong, London and New York. The Malaysian exercise, done while prices were depressed on the Kuala Lumpur Stock Exchange and in the midst of an economic recession, has restored some confidence to the Malaysian market and taken the pressure off the prices of the stocks concerned.

The market for big block deals has also been fuelled by the asset swaps of large corporations. When Guinness, the London-based brewing concern, took over the Distillers group after a bitter and controversial takeover struggle, it found itself with a block of 18.8 million British Petroleum (BP) shares. Some years earlier, Distillers had ended up with the BP block when it sold its chemical business to the British oil group. This block of shares had overhung the market for BP shares for some time after Guinness took control of the Distillers group. The way the new owners disposed of the shares is an illustration of the advances made in dealing with the placement of large blocks of shares.

Investors wanting to sell large blocks of shares are faced with several problems, the biggest being timing and pricing. Depending upon the tax regime, selling shareholders may seek to avoid too large or too immediate a hit from capital gains tax. Investment banks have been inventive enough to create various devices to circumvent these problems. Issuing a bond with warrants exchangeable into shares is one way of delaying the capital gain and therefore the tax associated with it. It also gives the shareholder cash almost immediately. Other investors have allowed merchant banks to create new financial vehicles to dispose of their shareholdings. A group of Arab investors holding Royal Dutch Shell shares had their stock packaged into a separate company. Warrants were then sold, giving the warrant holders the option to purchase the oil company's shares within a five-year exercise period. The Arab investors received a portion of the funds up-front while retaining control of the stock. Moreover, they had locked in the capital gain they would receive when the warrants are exercised. In the Guinness sale of BP shares, the sale was secured not so much through the creativity of the investment bankers concerned, but rather as a result of their muscle. The Guinness shares were 'bought' by Hoare Govett and Salomon Brothers for sale at $150 million. It took all of 90 minutes to distribute these shares among clients of the two securities houses.

The large amounts of capital deployed behind equity placements has encouraged some notably massive issues. When the Flick group wanted to sell off its Daimler Benz shares, it took the giant Deutsche Bank and a large consortium of banks, familiar with Eurobond distribution techniques, to spread the stock around the market. A similar operation in 1986 for Fiat, the Italian auto manufacturer, fared less well, with a confused market offered the same stock at several different prices. In retrospect, many felt the $1.6 billion deal might have been too big for the market. After all, the entire 1986 Euro-equity market was only approaching $12 billion at year end.

The intense mergers and acquisition market in the 1980s has also created large conglomerates seeking to raise cash through either the partial sale of subsidiaries or the disposing of shareholdings in related companies. In 1986, for instance, Credit Suisse First Boston lead managed an issue for Rupert Murdoch's Newscorp. The preference shares issued were exchangeable into fully paid 'B' shares of Reuters, the international news agency. A similar deal done for the Hong Kong group Jardine Matheson (now Bahama registered) allowed investors and holders of its preference shares to exchange them for shares in The Hongkong Land Company, perhaps the largest capitalized real estate company in the world. These two deals shared a common inspiration with an earlier IBM deal. When IBM wanted to sell off a large block of Intel shares, it used an exchangeable subordinated debenture to provide holders with a means to buy common stock in Intel.

Further refinement of the techniques for selling off large blocks without depressing prices was brought on by Banque Paribas Capital Markets, which recently arranged a $50 million 8% note issue for the French electronics group, Thomson-Brandt. The note is redeemable in 1996, but the attractive feature of the instrument is repayment in the form of shares in Thomson's subsidiary, Thomson-CSF, rather than the par value in cash. That meant the issuer could sell Thomson-CSF shares into the market at a premium rather than at a discount. The desire to sell shares at or above market, rather than at a discount, has driven sellers to use increasingly creative instruments.

The next step has been for intermediaries to create warrants, thus providing a whole new instrument for trading based on the underlying equity. The more creative institutions have been buying up parcels of shares, creating warrants and then selling them off, at the same time making a two-way market in these instruments. Increasingly, as the big block deals find themselves in the hands of foreign investors, it may also be possible for a large market to exist outside the home market. Already several stocks, long seasoned through trading among foreign institutions, enjoy foreign trading volumes as large if not larger than in their own domestic stock market. British chemicals group ICI can find itself more heavily traded in the United States on the American Depositary Receipt market than in London. Siemens finds a more liquid market for its markets in London than on its home exchange of Frankfurt.

Creative energies are also finding ways to circumvent the onerous registration rules of some European countries. In 1986, for instance, Swiss banks began creating warrants based on registered shares deposited with them. The warrants give investors a play on the underlying shares. The shareholders continue to receive dividend payments and only lose their shares when warrant holders exercise their option. Foreign investors can buy Ciba Geigy, Zurich Insurance and Nestlé shares in this manner. And the ultimate attraction is that, if the registered shares cannot be sold to a foreign holder and a Swiss investor cannot be found to take them up, the resulting fall in the warrants creates good arbitrage opportunities between the registered shares and the warrant market.

The private placement market is changing. It is no longer the discreet market where *ad hoc* deals were done on a 'best efforts' basis. The advent of the highly capitalized investment bank and broking house is changing the pace and character of the market. The successful firms will be those with a large capital base sufficient to buy and, if necessary, to warehouse large blocks of shares. These firms must also have a wide distribution network able to rapidly sell large blocks of shares. The days when brokers dealt on a best efforts basis, or shopped a parcel of shares around the market, is increasingly being overtaken by the use of both the bought deal and extensive networks encompassing big broking contacts and institutional clients. Indeed, the difference between block deals and syndicated offering is looking increasingly obscure. But the priorities for block placements remain the same. The primary requirement is still to sell shares at or above market price without adversely affecting the current share price. The difference today, however, is the vast variety of instruments and techniques available to the creative investment banker.

Chapter 3

Hybrid Equity Securities

Thomas Fairhead

Over the past two to three years, the Euro-equity element of the international equity market has, in many respects, emerged out of the market for hybrid securities. Indeed, an important part of the investor base for international equity issues has developed out of the long-standing market for convertible Eurobonds. As the market for international equity issues has taken off, however, there has been no corresponding decline in the issuing volume of hybrid securities. Rather, there has been a dramatic increase in the total volume of equity-related instruments that have been sold in the international capital markets between 1985 and 1987. While one part of this increase has consisted of straight equity issues, there has also been a dramatic increase in the volume of hybrid securities. Indeed, the volume growth of hybrid equity securities has outstripped even the dramatic growth in direct international equity offerings. While the Euro-equity market grew from $244 million in 1983 to $18 billion in 1987, in the same period the market for international hybrid equity securities grew from $4.8 billion to $38 billion.

Hybrid securities, as discussed here, cover primarily two groups of instruments. The first group are fixed rate instruments that carry a conversion option that allows the investor to convert or exchange their fixed rate investment, at a fixed price, into an equity security which gives the investor a direct participation in the earnings of the company. The second group comprises options and warrants to purchase shares at a stipulated price. These are issued either in a naked form or in a unit with a bond or other securities from which the warrants are then detachable. The investor pays a price for the option related to the market price of the underlying shares. The price paid often takes the form of a reduced coupon on the bond issue.

The existence of a significant market for both equity and varieties of hybrid equity securities means that both issuers and investors have a wide variety of alternatives to choose from when considering a primary market transaction. There are, typically, significant differences between the priorities of the issuer and those of the investor. On the one hand, the issuer is often most interested in the flexibility which the company has to use a single securities issue to meet a number of overall goals relating to its balance sheet, financing costs and other corporate objectives. On the other hand, an investor is typically reviewing alternative investments in terms of a break-even price at which one security becomes a more attractive vehicle for investment in a company than another.

Because the market for international equity issues has largely grown out of the corresponding Eurobond market, a significant proportion of the investment funds available are restricted to investment in debt or debt-related securities. In addition, therefore, to considering the relative benefits to an issuer of one type of security versus another, an issuer also has to consider the size of market to which it has access and the opportunities to tap different pockets of investment demand using different instruments. Similarly, there are limitations on the types of securities that different corporations may issue in their domestic markets and thus, in certain instances, there are greater attractions in tapping an international investor base to achieve the corporation's objectives.

INVESTMENT EVALUATION OF HYBRID SECURITIES

The investors' approach to a hybrid securities issue can be divided into two parts. First, are investors persuaded that the underlying shares of the company constitute an attractive medium-term investment? Second, do they consider that the hybrid securities represent an attractive (or, if their investment parameters are restrictive, the most attractive available) opportunity to invest in the underlying performance of the company's shares?

There are a variety of theoretical tools available to assist an investor when deciding whether the instrument on offer is more attractive than a direct equity investment. The best known and most widely used of these tools is the Black-Scholes option pricing model. This shows that the economic effects of owning an option are equivalent to a trading strategy involving a portfolio of shares and cash, where the proportion of the portfolio invested in shares varies according to the share price. Different trading strategies give a different effective exercise price. The 'theoretical value' of the option is equal to the cost of maintaining a trading strategy of this kind.

In practice, however, very few equity options markets trade on the basis of a Black-Scholes theoretical value. The most important markets that do use this model are the domestic short-term traded options markets in the United States and the United Kingdom. There is an important difference between the investment decision typically made by an international investor when offered a new issue and those made by an investor in these domestic short-term markets. The international market, while increasingly using Black-Scholes or comparable systems to establish the theoretical value of a hybrid security, continues to place much greater weight on the fundamental outlook for the shares.

In both the US and the UK, where there is widespread institutional shareholding, a typical institutional portfolio will contain a core of major investments in the important companies in their stock market. The portfolio is weighted in line with the constituents of the principal index by which the performance of the stock market is measured. Over time, an institution will increase or reduce its exposure relative to the indexed weightings depending on its expectations of the fundamental outlook for the companies concerned.

Thus, the institution is already familiar with the company involved and is likely to be a major shareholder. Its investment decision is therefore primarily based on whether an attractive arbitrage is offered by the hybrid securities being sold. Is it worthwhile for the institution to either increase its exposure to the shares, or replace part of its existing shareholding, by buying the equity option? It is, for example, a regular feature of US domestic convertible bond issues that, during the offer period for the convertibles, the market for the underlying shares comes under pressure. Institutions attracted by the terms of the convertible bond make space within their overall portfolis for the purchase of the securities. Similarly, in the UK, major institutions have begun to use the traded options market as a means of increasing or reducing their short-term exposure to a company's shares while at the same time retaining a fundamental core position which is hardly traded at all.

International investors, particularly the customers of the retail banks in continental Europe, do not have similar weighted core portfolios against which to assess the relative merits of a new hybrid security. The manager of such a portfolio will be concerned with the fundamental outlook for the company itself and his expectation of the share's performance.

With the Black-Scholes model, the benefits of owning shares versus the benefits of owning an equity option are assessed independently of any view on the underlying stock price. Indeed, for a long-term holder of the underlying shares, it may be highly attractive to have their potential downside risk limited by the ownership of options rather than common stock. An international investor who is deciding to buy the hybrid security is, however, at the same time making the fundamental investment decision to commit himself to the company. For this reason, companies whose share price history is highly volatile but which show little medium-term direction are often unable to achieve the value for a hybrid security that would be implied by a Black-Scholes model.

On the other hand, in markets which are considered undervalued or where there has been a significant level of price stability in the past, the value that the investor may be prepared to pay for a hybrid security may be substantially above the theoretical value. This may, for instance, occur when the fund in question is prohibited from direct share purchases. In addition, options are often attractive as a means of improving the overall return on an equity investment. Although this has no theoretical validity (in the Black-Scholes model an investor is assumed to have perfect access to finance for its portfolio), in practice most retail investment managers are prohibited by their clients from borrowing against their portfolios except in certain very restricted cases. Hence the 'gearing effect' is of real benefit.

OBJECTIVES FOR THE ISSUER

Issuers have an entirely different set of priorities and have increasingly found the international market highly attractive, partly because of the flexibility to structure securities to meet their specific requirements and partly because it gives them the opportunity to extend the overall base of investors available to support long-term financing needs. For any company considering issuing a significant amount of new equity securities, the fundamental concern will always be to protect the interests of existing shareholders as far as this is possible. This does not necessarily mean that all securities should be made available to those shareholders by pre-emptive rights. Rather, the terms at which any offering is done should not unreasonably dilute the value of existing shareholders' investments.

With the increasing concentration of shareholding in the hands of a relatively small number of institutions, the expected reaction of shareholders has come to play a greater role in the direct processes of corporate decision-making in capital market transactions. The experience of the past three years, which has seen the spread of hostile takeover activities from the United States and the UK to other markets around the world, has heightened the importance that management attaches to the maintenance of support among existing shareholders. In the long term, however, few companies consider it healthy to have a narrow shareholder base. Without a broad potential market for new share issues, a company is likely to be tightly constrained in its ability to take advantage of business opportunities. In addition, a company will always be under threat from a hostile bidder who is able to offer sufficient profits on shareholders' investment to induce investors to sell out. With recent increases in stock market values making it easier for companies to find investment opportunities which do not dilute the value of existing shareholdings, access to a broad market for their equities has become increasingly important.

With a volume of direct equity issues totalling $18 billion and hybrid equity securities totalling $38 billion in 1987, the international market has become increasingly important to the senior financial management of many corporations. For these senior officers, the international market is a potential answer to the problems of the inflexibility of their company's domestic market. While many companies may find it difficult to persuade their existing shareholders to further increase their exposure (which may already be substantially above the weighting that company has in the domestic market index), the same problem does not arise when dealing with new international investors. There has, therefore, been widespread interest in finding ways of placing corporate equity in the hands of the international investment community.

The problem is how best to do this. As already mentioned, a significant portion of investment funds is not available for direct investment in equity securities. The overall portfolios may contain some equity element but, for a large proportion of both retail and institutional funds in the international capital markets, the great preponderance of investment is in debt securities. If an issuer wants to develop a relationship with these investors that will eventually ensure that they become substantial equity investors, it is often found that the most successful introduction is made through the issuance of a hybrid security which ultimately carries the same source of investment return as a direct shareholding.

The fact that a significant part of the investment decision for an international investor, as opposed to a domestic investor, is made up of the fundamental analysis of the merits of the shares means that a hybrid issue does have the effect of extending the ultimate market for the shares. Investors buying a hybrid security have made a similar decision to an institution that makes a strategic move into a company's share capital. But they do so, not in response to an independent analyst's report, but because the company itself has gone out to seek, and issue new securities to, an additional investor base.

From the issuer's point of view, this investor base has a number of other attractive characteristics. Firstly, it contains a very large number of investors who are very widely distributed. Secondly, many of these investors become long-term core holders of investments that they purchase. They will not actively trade the securities or take short-term profits when they are available. In this, they are markedly different from the dealing portfolios of the domestic institutions who will form a significant part of the group of subscribers to any domestic offering.

This combination of relatively narrow liquidity and broad distribution of the securities means that a placement in the international markets is often a highly successful means of locking away shares or options on shares beyond the reach of a potential predator. There have been very few examples of market raids via hybrid securities in the international capital market. By contrast, there are numerous examples where domestic options markets have been used as a means to build up a strategic stake prior to a takeover bid. During 1986, against a background of hostile takeover bids, a number of convertible bond offerings were structured with put options designed to place the maximum possible number of shares in the hands of international investors.

The development of this market is important for most issuers not so much because of the terms that they are able to get in the first offering but rather because of the future opportunity for regular repeat issues in response to financing requirements. For example, there was a sequence of direct share offerings by Nestlé at successively higher prices during a five-month period in 1985. These offerings raised over $400 million, providing part of the financing for the Carnation acquisition. Similarly, the UK company BET followed up a convertible bond issue with a direct international placement of shares less than three months later. The most significant example to date, however, has been a financing programme totalling over $850 million by the Australian company Elders IXL, which was carried out in two stages in December 1986 and March 1987.

TECHNICAL ASPECT OF HYBRID SECURITIES ISSUES

In contrast to issues involving equity warrants, one important characteristic of convertible issues is the value of the call option. Most convertible issues carry a call option which can be exercised in the first three years of the bond's life, providing the share price has risen above some specified percentage of the conversion price. In almost all recent cases, this has been 130% of the conversion price. This call option effectively provides the issuer with an opportunity to force the holders of a convertible bond to exchange the bonds for direct equity in the company at a time of the company's choosing, assuming attractive share price performance. A large company may have a regular programme of small to medium-sized acquisitions which involve significant goodwill or other costs which require direct write-offs against its net assets. The ability to create a relatively small amount of new equity by calling the convertible bond issues provides a high degree of flexibility. This flexibility may not be available from direct equity offerings.

In the United States, for example, a direct equity offering will require registration and involve underwriting and other expenses which may either take too long or be too unwieldy to suit immediate corporate requirements. In the European markets, a direct share offering of any size would typically be offered first to the company's shareholders. Small issues may be cumbersome or inconvenient to administer. Moreover, such issues may undercut shareholders' support at a time when senior financial management are absorbed in negotiating the terms of an acquisition. The opportunity to force existing investors to convert from debt to equity may be significantly more attractive. This has a double effect on the company's gearing ratio by simultaneously both reducing outstanding borrowings and increasing equity.

For issuers who are concerned about earnings dilution or expecting substantial long-term improvement in the market for their shares, the opportunity for a deferred equity issue at a premium to the existing share price is often attractive. The classic example is the use of a convertible or equity warrant issue to finance the repurchase of outstanding shares. For instance, in 1984 when Texaco was forced by the Bass brothers to repurchase a significant stake in the company at a price above the then prevailing market levels, the repurchase was financed by the issuance of convertible bonds with a conversion price well above the then all-time high for the shares. This raised a total of $1500 million. Similarly, when a major strategic stake of W.R. Grace came on the market following the dismemberment of the Flick family holdings in 1986, W.R. Grace took the opportunity to repurchase these shares and finance the repurchase in part by issuing a convertible with a premium 44% above the repurchase price.

In both these cases, the transactions resulted in a net reduction in the number of shares or options on shares that were outstanding and, therefore, far from diluting existing shareholders interest, were in fact anti-dilutive. In exchange for giving up a premium price at which shares will become available to them, investors naturally receive a higher current yield. The return, however, is paid to them in the form of debt interest, not as dividends on shares. In certain recent offerings, there have also been a few variations in which this distinction has been somewhat blurred.

Because interest charges are deductible against current income for tax purposes, in a great number of cases the current after tax cost of the financing can be significantly lower than the cash cost of the dividends. In almost all respects, therefore, a hybrid equity security is likely to offer a corporate issuer a financing opportunity which is attractive when directly compared against an equity offering. Tax treatment varies widely and, in certain cases, notably for issuers domiciled in some offshore financial centres (and, in a very specific case, in the perpetual floating rate note market), there may be little difference between the tax treatment of debt and those issues with the economic characteristics of preference shares. Some examples during 1986 included the use of exchangeable preference shares by both Jardine Matheson and News Corporation as a means of placing part of their investments in certain major affiliates (in Jardine Matheson's case, Hongkong Land, and in News Corporation's case, Reuters), which provided them with new equity proceeds while at the same time keeping effective control of these investments in the hands of the issuers.

ALTERNATIVE STRUCTURES OF THE HYBRID SECURITY

The two most important considerations in deciding what type of security to issue have been the need for flexibility in matching the currency to the issuer's needs and, separately, the size of the transaction that is envisaged. Many issuers find that the most attractive terms available to them come from markets where the debt element of the hybrid security carries a liability denominated in a currency which is not attractive to the company. These issuers will want an opportunity to use the currency and interest rate swap markets to reorganize the liability on the debt to match the nature of their assets. Because a convertible bond issue may be converted at any time and an issuer who enters into a swap contract may therefore find himself with significant refinancing liabilities at off market rates, it is normally considered unacceptable to swap a convertible bond issue.

Where swaps will be needed, therefore, bonds with equity warrants attached are the normal securities chosen. The equity warrants will be traded separately from the bonds and, on the issuer's balance sheet, will be treated entirely separately. On exercise, they would represent new equity of the company but would not simultaneously involve a reduction in the company's outstanding debt. With certainty as to the ultimate maturity of the debt, it is then possible for the issuer to enter into a swap contract as required to match their funding requirement.

There are certain disadvantages with this procedure. Firstly, swap contracts, even if the underlying debt is subordinated, normally rank with senior debt. In addition, because the debt element of the package will often be sold to a different group of investors from the equity warrants, any difficulties an issuer may have in placing subordinated debt instruments will affect its equity warrant issue. Convertible issues, on the other hand, are often subordinated in nature. Secondly, because the debt instruments are, to a significant extent, placed with classic Eurobond investors, the size of an offering is limited by the size of the market for the issuer's debt securities when compared directly against debt securities of other issuers trading in the current primary market. For really large issues, such as those for Texaco or for Elders, it has normally been preferable to use convertible bonds which can be targeted to a number of regional submarkets and will not be treated as interchangeable commodities. The ultimate example of this was the Elders convertible issue in March 1987 in which no fewer than five separate currencies were used for the denomination of the convertibles in order to separately tap a wide variety of investor groups.

The volume of hybrid securities issues in the international capital markets shows little sign of abating. As an alternative to direct equity offerings, the importance of this market to both issuers and investors is clearly being recognized by a wider and wider group of participants. Besides playing a path-breaking role in the primary market, establishing a basis for the subsequent dramatic growth in the market for direct international equity issues, hybrid equity securities also remain the largest source of funds in the equity sector of the international capital market.

FOR FURTHER INFORMATION

1   J. C. Cox and M. Rubinstein, *Options Markets*. The basic reference book on option pricing theory and models.
2   T. Fairhead, 'The Use of Exchangeable Preference Shares in the Euromarket', *The Treasurer* magazine (March 1987).
3   T. Fairhead, 'Equity-Linked Financing for Adia S.A.', *The Treasurer* magazine (February 1986).

Chapter 4

Rule 415

Larry Kimmel

Thursday, 7 October 1982, was a day that perfectly illustrated the revolutionary changes taking place in Wall Street's capital markets. In a recent speech, Morgan Stanley president Robert Baldwin recalled what happened: 'We came to work with no issues on the calendar for the day. By the time we shut down, 18 issues had been sold. We had made nine separate bids. We had bought an issue for a company which had never done business with us before and one of our clients had accepted a competitor's bid; $1.9 billion of securities were sold. The long bond moved 28 basis points and the stock market at the same time rose 22 points on a turnover of 147 million shares.'[1]

With the introduction of Rule 415, corporations issuing securities in the United States gained much of the freedom enjoyed by issuers in the Eurodollar market. They can respond far more quickly to market opportunities, selling their securities in almost any way they like. Instead of going through a team of underwriters and negotiating a price at the end of the selling period, they can solicit firm bids to purchase the securities in advance, along the lines of a 'bought' deal in the Euromarkets. They can even sell stock direct to investors, cutting out the middleman altogether. Investment bankers are now confronted by an increasingly transaction-oriented marketplace.

As interest rates change throughout the world, issuers seek the lowest cost marketplace for raising funds. As the rules are relaxed so underwriters can compete on a level playing field, these corporations no longer see much difference between the US, Euro and Japanese capital markets. To better service these companies, investment bankers are expanding their capabilities worldwide. According to Robert Baldwin, one reason for this international push is that 'the dollar markets have become truly international as a result of 415. There are no longer important differences between the US and the Euro-dollar market. Issuers can go both ways – and do'.[2]

The Securities and Exchange Commission Rule 415, part of the Securities Act of 1933, provides provisions for the 'shelf registration' of securities. The rule permits eligible companies to use Form S-3 to register debt or equity securities. These securities can then be offered at any time during the next two years

26

without the need to file a new registration statement for each sale. 'Shelf registration' is so named because of a company's ability to put securities on the shelf (register) and then pull them off (underwriting) whenever the company so chooses. Only securities that are reasonably expected to be offered and sold within the two-year period can be registered. Rule 415 went into effect on a trial basis in March 1982 and, with some modifications, became permanent on 31 December 1982. The purpose of Rule 415 was to simplify the registration of new corporate securities and allow more flexibility in the way issues are underwritten.

BACKGROUND

The stock market crash of 1929 caused tremendous losses among the investing public and led to a series of laws designed to protect investors. Among these laws was the Securities Act of 1933, enacted to compel the disclosure of relevant factual information to investors. The act relates primarily to the initial distribution of securities rather than secondary trading (covered by the Securities Exchange Act of 1934). The Securities Act of 1933 had two principal purposes. Firstly, it mandates full and fair disclosure to potential investors of essential information about new securities sold through either interstate commerce or through the mail. The law requires that a registration statement be filed with the Securities and Exchange Commission (SEC) and that a prospectus be distributed to potential investors. Secondly, the law protects investors against fraud caused by omissions of material facts or misrepresentations. This objective is implemented by the use of both civil and criminal sanctions. The SEC may stop improper practices through the use of injunctions and may secure compliance with registration requirements through its power to issue stop orders.

The act does not give the SEC authority to pass judgment on the merits of securities. The act is based on the doctrine of 'caveat emptor' – let the buyer beware. As long as a true picture of the company is presented, the law does not stop the sale of securities by a worthless company. For example, over the last two or three years, there have been many offerings of the 'blind trust' variety. The issuer has no ongoing business, nor even a promising idea for a start-up company. The issuer is merely asking other people to give him money so that he may start a company when he thinks of a good idea. In almost all blind trust offerings, the officers intend to receive a salary for their efforts, even if they find no business avenues to invest in. No offering, no matter how worthless, will be prohibited by the SEC as long as all of the material facts are made known to the investing public.

The concept of shelf registrations was not a totally new procedure originating in 1982, although its use prior to this date was quite limited. Section 6(a) of the act states: 'A registration statement shall be deemed effective only as to the securities specified therein as proposed to be offered.' The SEC had always interpreted this clause to mean those securities which were to be offered in the immediate future and which were specifically described in the registration statement. It was thought that definitive security quantities and prompt issuance would assure investors that both registration statements and prospectuses contained current information about the issuing company.

The Securities Act of 1933 was designed to curtail the practice of high pressure sales tactics coupled with the sale of a new issue within a matter of days. Congress believed that lengthening this period would allow investors to learn about the issuing company and come to understand its merits. To this end, Section 5 of the act establishes three distinct stages in the registration process, the pre-filing period, the waiting period and the post-effective period. The ground rules for making offers and sales differ greatly in each of these three stages. The rules cover permissible conduct from the time a prospective issuer and underwriter agree to offer a new security through until after the distribution has been completed.

In the prefiling period, before a registration statement is filed with the SEC, the act prohibits the use of interstate facilities or the mail to offer or sell securities. Underwriting allotments can be made, but banks cannot be told exactly how many securities they will be asked to sell. Press releases, news articles and speeches can be construed to be 'offers' under the act. For example, in the often cited *SEC* v. *Arvida* case, underwriters issued press releases announcing the proposed offering of common stock to the public before filing a registration statement with the SEC.[3] The underwriters also released a description of the new company and plans for Arvida's development of real estate in Florida. This press release was considered an offer and therefore found to be a violation of Section 5(c) of the act.

The waiting period is the time between the filing of a registration statement and the statement becoming effective. At least 20 days was required to allow the SEC time to review the registration statement and for investors to receive information about the issuer. Amendments to the registration statement started this waiting period anew. Since the SEC often asked that additional information be provided to investors, the typical waiting period was well over 30 days. An underwriter could petition the SEC to accelerate the waiting period if adequate information had been provided to the public. During the waiting period, sales are still prohibited, but oral and written offers (via a preliminary prospectus called a 'red-herring') are allowed. The 'red-herring' prospectus gets its name from the red legend running along the left side of the cover page. Unlike the final prospectus, the preliminary prospectus does not contain underwriting and pricing information. Rule 134 of the Securities Act of 1933 prescribes norms for advertising. A tombstone advertisement, the usual form, contains the issuer's name, tentative date of issue, names of managing underwriters and a warning that the offering can be made only by means of a prospectus. During the waiting period, a due diligence meeting takes place between the issuer and the underwriters to review the prospectus and registration statement, and to address any formal SEC letters of comment or criticisms. During this meeting, underwriters have the opportunity to question the issuer and make certain all relevant information has been disclosed.

In the post-effective period, after the SEC declares the registration statement effective, sales can be freely made. Offers are limited by Section 5(b) of the act, which requires that purchasers of securities be furnished with a copy of the final prospectus prior to, or accompanying, the written offer or confirmation.

The traditional underwriting process thus involved the following steps:

- Issuer decides it needs additional capital.
- Preliminary negotiations take place between the issuer and managing underwriter(s) to work out the tentative terms of the offering.
- Counsels for the issuer and underwriters draft the registration statement and prospectus. The company's accountants prepare financial statements.
- After the registration statement is filed with the SEC, underwriters begin distributing the red-herring prospectuses.
- Attorneys for the underwriters file a copy of the registration statement in various states to obtain permission to sell in each state. This procedure is necessary under the 'blue-sky' statutes of each state.
- The SEC issues its letter of comment and amendments are made to the registration statement.
- Final price amendments are filed with the SEC and the offering is declared effective.
- Sales of securities are consummated.
- The closing takes place between the issuer and underwriters, with securities exchanged for the sale proceeds.

RULE 415

On 10 November 1983, the SEC announced the adoption of Rule 415, covering the registration of securities to be offered or sold on a delayed or continuous basis.[4] The rule was made available for offerings qualified to use short form registration statements (Forms S-3 or F-3) and for traditional underwritings. Securities may only be registered in an amount which, at the time the registration statement becomes effective, is reasonably expected to be offered and sold within two years from the initial effective date of registration.

The SEC decided to limit the availability of shelf offerings to primary offerings of debt and equity securities registered on Form S-3 or F-3, because these securities and issuers are considered to be of investment grade. The SEC believed that other, lower quality issuers or securities lacked adequate disclosure and needed extensive due diligence. For companies in the top tiers of investment quality, the SEC believed there was a steady stream of corporate information which was broadly disseminated and read. In addition, investors would be further protected by written procedures for conducting due diligence investigations and the adoption of an integrated disclosure system.[5] The eligibility requirements for Form S-3 must be met by *both* the issuer and the securities.

To be eligible for shelf registration, the aggregate market value of voting stock held by non-affiliates must be at least $150 million. This is the 'float test'. An *alternative float test* is acceptable where the aggregate market value of voting stock held by non-affiliates is $100 million or more, so long as the annual trading volume is at least three million shares. Even if neither of the above float tests is met, Rule 415 still permits 'investment grade' debt securities and non-convertible preferred stock to be registered on Form S-3. A security is considered of 'investment grade' if at least one nationally recognized rating organizations has rated the security in one of its four highest rating categories. The nationally recognized rating organizations would include Standard and Poor's, Moody's Investors Services, Fitch Investors Services and Duff and Phelps. If non-affiliated persons wish to make a secondary offering of existing shares, this is only allowed if the same class of securities is listed on a national exchange or quoted on NASDAQ. A primary offering of equity securities must not exceed 10% of the aggregate market value of the issuer's outstanding voting stock.

Prior to Rule 415, delayed offerings were permissible under certain circumstances, including secondary offerings by persons other than the registrant, its subsidiary or its parent; securities issued upon the exercise of outstanding options, warrants or rights; securities issued upon conversion of other outstanding securities; depositary shares evidenced by ADRs registered on Form F-6; and mortgage related securities. After the adoption of Rule 415, these types of offerings could continue to be made on a delayed basis.

BENEFITS AND DISADVANTAGES

The principal benefit that shelf registration provides is the lower issuing costs for corporations. Several empirical studies conclude that securities sold under Rule 415 have lower issuance costs than securities not sold under the rule. A recent study by Kidwell, Marr and Thompson concluded that debt issues sold under Rule 415 sell at between 30 and 40 basis points lower than comparable negotiated sales.[6] Competitively sold bonds resulted in a possible interest-cost savings of about 26 basis points for shelf-registered issues. The study found no evidence that interest-cost savings for shelf-registered issues varied between different bond credit rating classes.

A second study by Bhagot, Marr and Thompson indicated the issuing cost for equity securities sold under Rule 415 is about 13% less than that for comparable syndicated equity securities not sold under Rule 415 and 51% less for non-syndicated.[7] For a \$58.8 million stock issue (the average in their sample), this is equal to a cost savings of either about \$370 000 or \$800 000 an issue, depending upon whether the issue is syndicated or non-syndicated. This second study also addressed the 'market overhang' theory which states that the announcement of a new equity offering depresses share prices. According to the theory, the larger the issue size, the larger the drop in share price.[8] The findings of the Bhagot study did not support the market overhang argument, nor did the study find that shelf registrations depress stock prices more than traditional registrations.

Shelf registration leads to greater flexibility as well as lower costs. Under Rule 415, offerings can be timed to take advantage of favourable market conditions. Before Rule 415, each new security offering had to be registered separately. The required minimum delay was 48 hours between the decision to make an offering and the actual sale. An issuer can now ask for competing bids from its investment bankers and then sell securities immediately. This flexibility is important in today's volatile markets. A registrant can launch an offering during the most favourable market conditions. By taking advantage of 'market windows', registrants can obtain lower interest rates on debt, lower dividend rates on preferred stocks and higher prices on common stock.

Registrants are also able to vary the structure and terms of securities quickly so that they can meet the current demands of the marketplace. This freedom has spawned creative financings such as zero coupon bonds, floating rate coupons, bonds with interest rate caps and bonds which have put provisions for its holders and call provisions for issuers. Before Rule 415, each modification to an issue necessitated that a separate amendment be filed with the SEC. Simplifying the registration statement has also lowered fixed costs. Legal, accounting and printing costs have been cut because now only a single registration statement need be filed for a series of offerings. There are no accurate estimates of dollar savings brought about by Rule 415, but former SEC Chairman John Shad estimates the savings in paperwork to be \$300 million per year or about \$50 000 per issue.[9]

But Rule 415 has shortcomings, as Salomon Brothers Chairman John Gutfreund made clear in testimony before the SEC. He voiced industry concern that underwriters cannot make as thorough an appraisal of the quality of disclosure: 'One example of effective underwriter's due diligence was in connection with Penn Central, shortly before its demise in 1970. I was among those personally involved in that matter. During the process of preparing the offering circular, a process which extended over several weeks and in which underwriters and their counsel were actively involved, new facts were brought to light about the financial condition of the company. It was an episode where our industry stood firmly to protect the public investor.' If today's rules were in effect in 1970, Penn Central Co. would have qualified for use of short Form S-3 prospectus. No business information would have been included, and there would have been nothing in the prospectus of a substantive nature on which to perform due diligence. The marketplace, including investors, underwriters and dealers, would have relied on previous 1934 Act filings prepared by Penn Central. It is questionable whether the underwriter would have discovered problems with Penn Central under today's instantaneous shelf procedures.[10]

Due diligence refers to the investigation performed by underwriters prior to a public offering. The underwriters are obligated to ensure that there are no misstatements or omissions in the registration statement. Section 11 of the Securities Act makes underwriters liable for improprieties and errors in registration or distribution unless they have made reasonable efforts to check on the registration statement. Rule 415 drastically reduces the time available for an underwriter to investigate disclosures made in the registration statement. It is impractical for a potential underwriter to devote the time and expense necessary to conduct a due diligence review before knowing whether it will be selected to handle an offering. The SEC has adopted Rule 176 which addresses concerns of underwriters with respect to their liability under Section 11 of the Securities Act (1933) for information contained in incorporated documents. Rule 176 lists several factors for a court to consider in connection with a claim under Section 11, including the circumstance of incorporation. Were the documents prepared without the assistance of the underwriters? What information about the issuer was available to the investment banks concerned? It is clear that Rule 176 does not alleviate basic statutory due diligence obligations of underwriters.

Since the first Rule 415 shelf offering in May 1982, more than half of all new debt issues and one third of new equity offerings have come to market without the benefit of a syndicate, according to Securities Data Co. For an issue of $250 million of 20 year, 7⅛% GMAC debentures in 1972, no fewer than 173 firms were recruited for the syndicate. From start to finish, the whole underwriting process took three weeks and required 1000 or more telephone calls.[11] Contrast this with another $250 million GMAC offering in April 1984. Acting on the spur of the moment to take advantage of a suddenly receptive market, GMAC solicited competitive bids from its four designated underwriters and selected First Boston to handle the whole four-year note issue. The investment bank put up its own capital to buy the whole issue. It sold the notes almost exclusively to its own institutional clients.[12] The entire process took less than one day.

Several factors have led to the decline of the syndicate and the concentration of the largest deals in the hands of relatively few underwriters. Windows in the marketplace force issuers to sell their securities quickly. This can often only be accomplished through using a small number of firms. With the advent of smaller syndicates, only the most highly capitalized firms are willing to risk buying huge amounts of securities either alone or jointly with a few other firms. Moreover, in order to compensate themselves for thinner underwriting spreads, underwriters need to sell larger quantities of securities to maintain profit levels.

In a study conducted by Rogowski and Sorensen, they tracked the top ten

Table 4.1: *Concentration of total corporate securities underwriting*

	Top five investment banks		Top ten investment banks	
	Amount* ($ million)	%	Amount ($ million)	%
1979	22.730	62.1	30.358	82.9
1980	35.623	59.1	50.166	83.2
1981	40.760	63.7	53.446	83.5
1982	42.782	54.1	55.637	70.5
1983	54.592	56.1	76.675	78.8
1984†	71.669	74.7	82.849	86.3

Source: Directory of Corporate Financing, Investment Dealers'
Digest, and Institutional Investor.
* Full credit given to lead manager.
† Jan.–Oct. 1984.

investment banks from 1979 through 1986.[13] As shown in Table 4.1, the leading firms were able to take market share away from other investment banks at an increasing rate in 1983 and 1984. The trend towards underwritings by fewer and larger firms continued in 1985 and 1986. Table 4.2 shows that the top five firms managed 70.4% of all issues in 1985 and 66.1% in 1986. Statistics for the top ten firms reveal that these banks managed 90.7% of issue volume in 1985 and 89.3% in 1986.

With the time-consuming and cumbersome process of syndication now on the decline, investment banking firms must become more aggressive in seek-

Table 4.2: *The leading underwriters (full credit to book manager)*

Manager	1986 Amount ($ millions)	Rank	%	Issues	1985 Amount ($ millions)	Rank	%	Issues
Salomon Brothers	51 028.3	(1)	17.9	450	30 898.2	(1)	22.3	293
First Boston	44 096.1	(2)	15.5	406	21 572.7	(2)	15.6	274
Morgan Stanley	31 819.6	(3)	11.2	275	10 050.1	(6)	7.3	104
Drexel Burnham Lambert	30 732.2	(4)	10.8	266	13 336.7	(5)	9.6	171
Merrill Lynch	30 537.7	(5)	10.7	313	15 375.9	(4)	11.1	188
Goldman, Sachs	29 456.4	(6)	10.3	267	16 365.1	(3)	11.8	145
Shearson, Lehman Bros.	17 512.7	(7)	6.1	281	9 609.5	(7)	6.9	164
Kidder, Peabody	10 153.5	(8)	3.6	186	3 829.2	(8)	2.8	83
Paine Webber	5 048.9	(9)	1.8	125	2 920.5	(9)	2.1	74
Bear, Stearns	4 087.5	(10)	1.4	85	1 320.4	(14)	1.0	30
Prudential-Bache	4 073.4	(11)	1.4	77	1 346.9	(13)	1.0	41
Smith Barney	3 465.4	(12)	1.2	64	1 639.0	(10)	1.2	37
Dean Witter Reynolds	2 419.5	(13)	0.8	48	1 417.5	(11)	1.0	33
E. F. Hutton	2 341.1	(14)	0.8	43	955.6	(15)	0.7	24
Lazard Frères	2 198.7	(15)	0.8	15	740.6	(17)	0.5	11
Industry Totals	285 331.8			3767	138 287.9			2 222

Source: Investment Dealers' Digest (12 Jan. 1987).

ing business and more willing to assume greater amounts of risk. Companies with a large capital base and with wide institutional distribution capabilities have flourished. The successful firms have exhibited strong market knowledge. Firms need to be active in all segments of the secondary markets to structure an offering at the lowest cost to the issuer. Proven distribution capability on the part of investment banks is particularly important to those issuers who want their securities sold widely. It is also important that the purchasers hold these securities rather than quickly selling them back into the marketplace, thus deflating the price of an equity offering. Moreover, firms need to have sufficient capital and be willing to purchase huge amounts of securities at a moment's notice. Increased market volatility means investment bankers must provide immediate capital commitments whenever there is a favourable window in the marketplace. But detecting market opportunities is not enough. Firms must also be able to appraise the relative values between different markets and different securities. With the increasing competition between the top firms, an innovative investment bank may well be able to provide an issuer with the lowest capital cost. Block trades are becoming a more prevalent form of new issue distribution. Single-handed and two-handed deals are no longer unusual. Underwriters must be able to purchase equity securities and resell them to customers without adversely affecting the existing market. Finally, firms must have ongoing contacts with their clients to better understand their financing needs. Competition may be more intense, but issuers will often choose the investment bank with which they are most familiar.

Notes

1   Richard Lambert, 'Greater Initiative in International Risk-Taking', *Financial Times*, (8 Dec. 1982).
2   Ibid.
3   *SEC* v. *Arvida*, 169 F Supp 211 (S.P. N.Y. 1958).
4   SEC Release no. 33–6499 (23 Nov. 1983).
5   SEC Release no. 33–6383 (3 Mar. 1983) and Release no. 33–6437 (19 Nov. 1982).
6   David S. Kidwell, M. Wayne Marr and G. Rodney Thompson, 'SEC Rule 415: The Ultimate Competitive Bid', *Journal of Financial and Quantitative Analysis*, vol. 19 no. 2 (June 1984).
7   Sanjai Bhagat, M. Wayne Marr and G. Rodney Thompson, 'The Rule 415 Experiment: Equity Markets', *Journal of Finance*, vol. XL no. 5 (Dec. 1985).
8   Ibid.
9   S. Hodes, 'Shelf Registration: the Dilemma of the Securities and Exchange Commission', *Virginia Law Review*, vol. 49 (1983).
10   John Gutfreund, 'The Salomon Position on Rule 415', *The Market Chronicle* (22 July 1982).
11   Beth Selby, 'The Twilight of the Syndicate', *Institutional Investor* (Aug. 1985).
12   Ibid.
13   Robert J. Rogowski and Eric H. Sorensen, 'Deregulation in Investment Banking: Shelf Registrations, Structure and Performance', *Financial Management* (spring 1985).

Chapter 5

The Canadian Bought Deal

Cheryl I. Leonhardt

In May 1984, the Royal Bank of Canada issued C$100 million in floating rate first preferred shares. The issue was single handedly purchased and taken to market by Gordon Capital Corp. The era of the Canadian bought deal had begun. From May 1984 to September 1986, 52.68% of the dollar volume of all Canadian issues were bought deals. In the same period, bought deals accounted for 34.92% of the dollar volume for common stock and common equity unit issues. Traditional underwriting approaches are now being replaced by an increasingly competitive method of investment dealing which is putting strains on the Bay Street investment fraternity.

With a bought deal, a single investment house or a syndicate of dealers purchase stocks or bonds at a firm price and then resells them to investors. The issue is purchased by the investment dealer or dealers before the preparation of any disclosure documentation relating to the issuer or the securities involved, and before any specific canvass of the marketplace. All market risk is shifted to the underwriter or underwriting group which guarantees the issuer its money. The deal is confirmed immediately since no prospectus filing nor securities commission clearance is required, though a prospectus must be filed at a later date.

By contrast, the traditional approach to issuing equity in Canada involves the filing of a preliminary prospectus, the subsequent filing of a final prospectus and then the public distribution of the document. A preliminary prospectus is required under the Ontario Securities Act (1980). In the period from the initial filing to final approval, typically a month in duration, the underwriter canvasses the market to ascertain the extent of purchase interest. When the final prospectus is approved, a firm price proposal is presented to the issuer and dealers are able to confirm their sales. Given the prior investigation of the marketplace in premarketing efforts, the risk to the underwriter is minimal. The lengthy nature of this process militated against the bought deal.

In 1982, securities commissions across Canada adopted the prompt offering prospectus (POP) qualification system which allows senior companies to file a short form prospectus as issue documentation. To qualify for prompt offering in the western provinces of Canada and in Ontario, the issuing corporation must have been a reporting issuer for 36 months, complied with all continuous disclosure requirements and filed an annual information form. In addition, the issuer must have an aggregate market value of listed equity shares of at least C$75 million and have either minimum consolidated shareholder's equity of C$100 million or after tax net income of at least C$15 million for two of the last three fiscal years. To qualify in Quebec, the reporting issuer must have satisfied continuous disclosure requirements for one year and have established a permanent information record with Quebec's Administrator, including the latest annual report and documents filed since the end of its last financial year.

The introduction of the POP system streamlines issue clearance and reduces the one-month clearance period associated with the traditional approach. The primary jurisdiction has only three days to give comments on the preliminary prospectus. All other commissions have an additional two days to comment. With this shorter approval time, the dealer has increased regulatory confidence when offering a firm bid for an issue prior to documentation.

In addition to the introduction of the POP system in 1982, the institutional cash reserve situation in 1981 and 1982 provided a hospitable environment for the introduction of the bought deal. Following the build up of cash reserves during the 1981/82 Canadian bear market, institutions were eager to invest these reserves when the stock market bottomed in August 1982 and subsequently started to rise. Institutional concern centred on investing and gaining returns in an attractive market rather than on the maintenance of secondary market liquidity. A receptiveness and, in fact, a demand for issues facilitated the quick placement of securities and increased the confidence of brokers in their placing ability. Continuing favourable markets and decreasing interest rates have sustained institutional interest. The bought deal, whose success rests on a brokerage firm's ability to quickly offload its issue liabilities, has thrived in this marketplace.

In instances where an underwriting group undertakes a bought deal, the lead-managing underwriter discusses the market for the issue with the issuer and recommends an issue package. The other underwriters are contacted, and asked to evaluate and agree to participate in the proposed deal. The lead underwriter then presents the proposal to the client who immediately, usually within one hour, accepts or rejects the proposal. No premarketing is undertaken prior to the firm bid by the underwriters. The bidding process is based wholly on the dealers' market judgment as to their ability to unwind the commitment. The entire transaction, frequently hundreds of millions of dollars in size, is consummated on an entirely verbal basis.

CHANGES IN THE INVESTMENT ENVIRONMENT

The bought deal has altered traditional syndicate relationships. Since 1984 more than 90% of POP issues have been bought deals. The 5% to 10% that have not been bought are new concept issues such as the recent 'zero strike warrants' offered by Crownx and Nova. The growing volume of bought deals has become concentrated in the hands of a few dealers who have the necessary capital and trading operations. The smaller syndicates and reduced revenues characteristic of bought deals no longer support as many small and middle-size firms. In addition, traditional underwriter–client loyalties have deteriorated with the increased competition for deals. Issuing corporations are now switching the emphasis away from a long-term service and support relationship and towards the evaluation of individual underwriters on a low price, deal by deal basis.

Issuing costs of underwritten equity offerings have also been altered. Issuing costs are comprised of the commission paid to the investment dealer for its services, the inhouse cost to the issuer in terms of accounting fees, filing fees and management time, and the opportunity cost incurred from any underpricing of shares. In a bought deal, the increased competition among dealers has decreased underwriting margins and generally decreased the commission paid by issuers. The issuer's cost of documentation is greatly reduced as few resources are employed before the deal is firm. By contrast, in a traditionally underwritten deal, company resources may be expended and the deal never completed. The risk of mispricing the securities offered in a bought deal rests entirely with the investment house which buys the issue. Should the market price rise, the differential accrues to the dealer and the opportunity cost of the issue rises. Conversely, should the market price fall, the issuer benefits. The dealer bears the total market risk and insulates the issuer from potentially large drops in the share price.

In a traditional deal, the price of the issue is not set until immediately before the filing of a final prospectus. No market stabilization by the dealer is undertaken until a receipt for the prospectus is received and a press release circulated. By the time the issue is priced, the market has already responded to the filing of the preliminary and final prospectus. Conversely, in a bought deal, the broker has committed itself to a price and has an incentive to maintain the market price of the stock at or above the agreed price level. The market may be unaware of the issue and have little information about the deal's size and price. When an underwriter is involved in distribution pursuant to a prospectus, it may take action to stabilize the market but may not uptick the stock. If there is a time delay between the price commitment by the dealer and selling the issue to clients, the risk that the price will change is higher. The market stabilization activities permissible in this case are small to nil.

With a traditionally underwritten deal, the underwriting agreement is not signed until immediately before the final prospectus is filed. At that time, the deal is priced and the issuer and dealer agree to broad protective clauses on which the dealer can rely should the issue become unprofitable or should the issuer fail to meet the necessary factual and legal requirements. In a bought deal, the dealer surrenders its traditional protection and commits itself to a firm price at the time of signing. From the dealer's perspective, the issuer has confirmed its understanding of the commitment through its cooperation in the preparation of documentation. From the issuer's point of view, the dealer has limited ability to terminate the contract. There is usually no 'market out' clause in a bought deal agreement.

With a bought deal, there are changes in the marketing effort by dealers. Premarketing, an integral stage in the traditional underwriting approach, is eliminated. The buyer of the deal relies on the perceived marketability of an issue and its own estimated placement ability to establish a reasonable price. Prompt placement of the issue is essential to minimize carrying cost and market exposure.

The purchase mix in the market may also be modified. The institutionalization of the market has increased since 1984 as institutions typically purchase larger blocks of stock and are more reliable than retail investors for both the quick placement of issues and prompt payment. The retail/institutional split on the purchase is, however, also partly determined by the nature of the equity. A stock which pays dividends has greater retail appeal in Canada. The institutional and retail split is exemplified in a recent bought deal of Falconbridge common equity units in which 70% was sold to institutions and 30% to retail investors, whereas a bought deal for Cominco's common equity was sold wholly to institutions. Issues for retail sale are purchased by underwriters at a discount of up to 5.50% to compensate for the increased cost of salespersons, administration and expenses. Consequently, although the issuer achieves wider equity distribution, the cost of capital rises. In addition, the distribution of bought secondary offerings often receives unexpectedly negative retail reactions.

RISKS AND BENEFITS

With bought deals, risks to the dealer are high. At the launch of an issue, dealers regularly hold securities worth C$25 million to C$50 million or more. In an estimated 60% of bought deals, full commission spread is maintained. A further 35% maintain 50% to 75% of the spread while the remainder sustain losses. The underwriting spreads on bought deals have decreased 10 to 20% compared with traditional issuing. The dealer bears the risk of calling a market without the advantage of either a preliminary prospectus or premarketing information about the distribution potential and the likely equilibrium price. After the deal is bought the total market risk rests with the dealer. To a limited degree, a dealer can engage in market stabilization to support the present stock price or limit any decrease. The dealer is, however, prohibited from upticking the stock to increase the market appeal of an issue.

The dealer bears the time risk of the issue, the risk that market conditions will deteriorate between purchase and distribution. Due to the lack of documentation prior to the completion of a deal, there is usually no 'market out' clause. If the market deteriorates and the position is not cleared the same day, carrying costs can be substantial. Further costs are incurred the longer the position is held. Typically, a short amount of time elapses between the underwriters agreeing to the terms and the issuer's response, and thus distribution is promptly achieved. When there is a long time delay, however, large losses can be incurred.

With a bought deal, the dealer is exposed to legal risk and bound by due diligence requirements and contractual obligations. The dealer's legal obligation of due diligence, ensuring full, true and plain disclosure of prospectus material, is of vital importance in an equity issue because equity is traded and priced on fundamentals. Under the POP system, dealers must exercise due diligence for all materials referred to in the short form prospectus. Given the scope of the materials and the time constraints in a bought deal, full examination may prove difficult. Dealers are, however, as liable as they would be in a normally marketed transaction.

After the deal is purchased, a brokerage firm can find itself in a dilemma. Once a contract is agreed, the dealer has both a statutory responsibility to effect due diligence and a contractual obligation to purchase and market the issue. In the case when a dealer feels that it cannot sign the prospectus due to the document's failure to meet disclosure requirements, the dealer must ascertain the materiality of this failure. Materiality can be defined as the ability to effect movement in a stock price. If the information is not deemed material and the dealer refuses to endorse the issue, then the dealer can be sued for breach of contract. Conversely, if the dealer signs the prospectus as a confirmation of acceptable disclosure and the information is deemed material, the dealer may be sued for investor damages. In such instances, skilful negotiation is needed to reach an agreement which preserves both parties' reputations in the marketplace while ensuring a successful issue.

Several aspects of bought deals reduce the dealer's overall risk. First, after the pricing and offering of an issue, the closing of the transaction is effected in a short period of time and the underwriter receives prompt payment. The risk that markets will change in this short time period is minimal. In addition, the market is dominated by professional institutional investors who will make payment even when the market deteriorates. The risk to the dealer's credit position is thus reduced.

Though the risks undertaken by dealers increase in the bought deal environment, the issuer's market risk on a deal by deal basis is alleviated. In the issuer's overall financing process, however, the onus to evaluate proposals and prices has shifted from the combined underwriter and issuer team in a traditional deal, to the issuer itself. In a traditional relationship, the two parties worked in cooperation, and underwriters provided free services and advice between financings. Given the competitive nature of bought deals, the issue's underwriter would have a conflict of interest if it advised the client as to the best deal while at the same time competing for the business. The onus has shifted to the issuer's internal department to understand, analyse and evaluate each financing proposal with a view to finding which proposal best fits the company's goals and offers a fair price. The lack of previous experience in unilateral financing decisions increases the possibility that the issuer may leave money on the table or fail to meet its financing objectives. The majority of issuing clients maintain good relations with the major dealers so that they can evaluate each broker's advice and adjust the composition of a deal's underwriters accordingly. In the future, issuers should expect to spend a larger portion of their finance budget in fees for financial advisory services as dealer spreads narrow and increased competition for business becomes the norm.

The bought deal has changed the rewards as well as the risks. The benefits accrue to a small group of dealers. Those with adequate capital are undertaking principal transactions and are gaining volume that they would not otherwise have attained. The larger firms are earning decreased commission fees on a per deal basis but the increase in transaction volume more than compensates, maintaining or increasing the total fees received. In Canada, the four major players, Dominion Securities Inc., Gordon Capital Corp., Wood Gundy Inc. and McLeod Young Weir Ltd., dominate the bought deal market. They also tend to syndicate among themselves to achieve retail distribution and further the concentration of deals in the hands of a few investment houses.

The issuing corporation is the principal beneficiary of the bought deal. In contrast to a traditional underwritten issue, the dealer bears all risk that adverse market conditions will render the proposed deal unfeasible. Once the issuer accepts the bidder's firm offer, price declines in the securities decrease the dealer's profitability on the issue while the issuer's cash flow from the deal remains unchanged. The cost of the issue to the issuer is reduced by the decreased underwriting spread associated with a bought transaction. Expenses are further diminished when a traditional underwriting syndicate is not required for distribution. In addition, the cost of issue documentation is reduced because no documentation is assembled until the deal is firm.

Among the other benefits are timeliness and flexibility. In a bought deal environment, an issuer can quickly take advantage of a favourable market for its securities, ensuring that the issue price is comparatively high. Due to the confidentiality of bought deals, the issuer can come to the market without public exposure. Such publicity may be undesirable depending on the company's situation and security price.

The bought deal environment has lead to increased concentration in underwriting volume. Several factors have contributed to the success of the firms who have achieved dominance in this issuing approach. A substantial capital base is essential. A major player must have the resources to purchase one or more deals and also absorb any losses should the market deteriorate. A strong trading operation is necessary to stabilize the market activity of the stock.

Sound market knowledge of the stock is needed in judging a reasonable striking point for a competitive bid. Even more important is the purchasing firm's ability consistently and effectively to market new issues so that any carrying costs are minimized. Given that equities are purchased and sold on fundamentals, a successful dealer will need current and credible research at its disposal to help the marketing effort.

Eurobond houses who are expanding into international equity distribution will probably experience difficulty if they participate in the Canadian bought deal market. To properly price an issue and effect quick marketing requires a strong Canadian base with sound market knowledge and fundamental research. Without these attributes, the risks undertaken by houses participating in the bought deal market would be unreasonable. But as the financial community moves towards a world equity market, and as international dealers establish stronger offices in Canada and around the globe with better research on a wider list of Canadian companies, the bought deal market will probably expand to include more international houses.

Chapter 6

Going Public Abroad: The Case of US Companies in the UK

Robert Swannell and Richard Lazarus

In this chapter we review the principal issues relating to initial public offerings (or 'flotations' in British parlance) by US companies in London. We consider the reasons why such issues have occasionally been subject to adverse treatment at the hands of the UK investment community and press, and discuss the necessary features for a US issue to achieve major success here. We have deliberately avoided getting too involved in the technical detail that concerns practitioners in order to concentrate on the major points involved.

The increasing globalization of markets should, in theory, reduce to irrelevance the choice of which market a company selects for its initial public offering (IPO). Since all major investors in each country have teams of analysts following each overseas market, one might reasonably predict that similar investment criteria should apply to buying stock in, say, a Dutch company, whether it was listed in the Netherlands, London or New York. Shares in such a company will be subject to largely the same concerns – industry risks, currency swings, prospects for future growth in earnings – wherever its investors are initially located, and in the long run one might plausibly expect the individual stock markets themselves to compete for IPOs of well run, fast growing companies.

To some extent, of course, this is happening. Many leading shares are traded heavily in a number of overseas markets. IPOs for foreign companies are far from unusual, and sophisticated investors buy stocks they expect to make money on, regardless of where they are listed. Overseas investors frequently have a major role in establishing the underlying market values of domestically listed shares (*vide* Glaxo). At present, however, it appears that London, for all its suspicions, is the most receptive of all the major capital markets to foreign IPOs.

And yet, and yet . . . none of this has quite worked to dispel the suspicions that foreign companies come to London following an unsuccessful effort to persuade their compatriots of their virtues. There has been a long and richly endowed tradition of foreign adventurers, perhaps particularly from the US, proving a less than rewarding experience for UK investors. The coincidence of cowboy hyperbole on the one hand, and naïve greed on the other, facilitated the initial financing of many of the Western hemisphere's railroads and mines; one might comment that this provides the oil ventures of the 1970s and 1980s with a traceable, if illegitimate, parentage.

Every new issue for any domestic or overseas entity raises certain basic issues as to why the company is going public, whether it is really a suitable vehicle for outside shareholders and whether the proprietors are only providing such investors with the privilege of participating in their company because they believe that it is now ex-growth. US issues, just the same as domestic issues in London, cannot avoid facing these obvious questions: but they also face other pressures. Compelling investment attractions are needed to persuade English and Scottish institutions to set aside any initial suspicions as to why the US company has come so far for its funding.

ADVANTAGES OF LISTING IN LONDON

So why should a US company with attractive growth prospects contemplate running the somewhat suspicious British investors' gauntlet? Is it worth it? The principal advantages (the priority ordering of which will vary according to the circumstances of the company concerned) are as follows:

International exposure

For a company with overseas aspirations, present or future, an IPO provides a golden opportunity to capitalize on the extensive publicity surrounding the flotation, to achieve other objectives and get the company known outside its host country. For Mrs Fields, as one example of companies brought to the UK market by Schroders in 1986, it unlocked access to prime sites in the UK on significantly better terms than hitherto and emphasized the international perspective of the company. For Borland, another such company, it provided ample scope for publicizing its software products in several European markets. While an Introduction (listing a company in London which is already listed elsewhere) can provide similar scope for financial public relations, a full offer for sale obviously achieves far more publicity and comment.

Initial cost

While listing in London is far from cheap, particularly in the context of an Offer for Sale and the requirements to publish the prospectus in full in the press, underwriting commissions at 2% are significantly less than typical underwriting spreads in the US. The cost of coming to the market by way of a placing, which is permissible provided the amount raised is less than £15 million, is even lower, at typically only 0.75%, since the 1.25% sub-underwriting commission is not required.

While US legal costs can often be exaggerated, New York securities lawyers have a far from benign reputation elsewhere in the US, and some of Schroders' US clients have been impressed at the relatively non-adversarial behaviour of our UK lawyers. Certainly, our solicitors regard part of their role in a flotation as helping to get the deal done at the minimum necessary cost in terms of professional advisers' time, and UK legal costs are significantly less than in the US. In addition to lawyers, the principal cost will be for the auditors and reporting accountants, the cost of which will vary significantly depending on the complexity of the group and any restructuring required prior to flotation. In Table 6.1 we set out an estimate of costs of a UK IPO for a US company. This should obviously be treated with some caution since circumstances (and hence costs) vary considerably.

Table 6.1: *Indicative expenses for the UK flotation of a US company on the USM or the main market (£ thousands)*

	USM		Main market	
	Placing	Offer for Sale	Placing	Offer for Sale
Advertising*	5	5–180	5	65–200
Sponsor	100–200	100–200	100–200	100–200
Broker	25–35	25–35	25–35	25–35
Accountants†	40–90	40–90	50–100	50–100
Lawyers – UK	40–80	50–100	40–80	50–120
Lawyers – US	20–40	20–40	20–40	20–40
Printing	50–60	50–100	50–60	60–100
Design	6	8	6	8
PR consultancy	20	20	20	20
Registrars/receiving bankers	5	10–15	5	15–20
Initial listing fee (depending on market capitalization)	7	7	15	15
Contingency	30–50	40–80	30–60	60–100
	348–598	375–875	366–626	488–958
Plus Commission (including sub-underwriting commission and fees to brokers) as a percentage of funds raised	0.75–1.0%	2.0–2.25%	0.75–1.0%	2.0–2.25%

* Minimum advertising requirement for a USM Offer for Sale is one formal notice; for marketing purposes, however, full publication of the prospectus in at least one national newspaper, and possibly two, will generally be regarded as essential. Figures shown for placings assume that two distributors are used to effect the marketing, obviating the need for full publication of a prospectus in a national newspaper.

† Accounting costs vary enormously, depending upon the complexity of the company involved, number of subsidiaries and quality of records. Certain flotations have involved costs of up to $500 000 for reporting accountants/auditors.

Ongoing costs

Certain costs of being listed in London may well exceed the comparable costs of being listed in the US: any US client of Schroders who lists in London would be expected to come to London for every major announcement, including interim and final results, and to be available to face questions from analysts and the press. On the other hand, the UK market benefits from a relatively centralized structure for the dissemination of information. Few companies are followed by more than 10 to 15 analysts, and almost all the major institutional investors in the London market will be aware of the projections published by each analyst in respect of all the companies he/she follows. This enables investors nation-wide to keep abreast of changing market expectations with relative certainty, and without every listed company needing to employ an investor relations staff to handle calls from analysts. This differs significantly from US practice, where a broker in Minneapolis or Houston would not routinely have access to re-search material published in New York.

Rating

UK investors will be sensitive to the valuation which would be accorded a US company coming to the London market, if it were listed in the US, and will be reluctant to pay a premium over the level at which similar companies are rated by US investors in the US domestic market. Coming to London should not of itself merit such a premium, and theoretically there should be no arbitrage opportunities between markets. Nonetheless, the familiarity of the London market with the practice of formally valuing companies on the basis of prospective rather than historic or trailing 12 month earnings may provide a fast growing company with scope for accelerating the achievement of a specific level of valuation, from, say, three months after the year-end to between three and six months beforehand. While US investors acquire shares on the basis of expectations, just as they do in the UK, a formal profit forecast reported on by accountants and merchant bankers in the UK provides a mechanism for treating future profits as if they were more or less guaranteed, and valuing the company accordingly.

Size

To a very modest extent, a small US company might take the view that if it listed in the US, it would achieve very little impact, while by listing in London it attracts much more coverage. We doubt whether this is of itself much of an advantage unless the company has specific reasons for seeking publicity over-seas.

Disclosure

Perhaps the weakest reason for coming to the UK, and one which is of only very restricted validity, is the commonly expressed belief that UK disclosure requirements are less stringent than those imposed by the Securities and Exchange Commission (SEC) in the US. We take the view that the overriding duty of a UK sponsor is to ensure that potential investors have all the information they need to make an intelligent decision as to whether to invest or not. While commercially sensitive information which the SEC would require to be published is sometimes of little interest to an investor, one way or the other, the converse is far more often the case.

ACHIEVEMENT OF A SUCCESSFUL ISSUE

Most of the same attributes apply to a US company coming successfully to the London market as they would to a domestic UK issue. While there has been a reasonable proportion of disasters amongst US companies making IPOs in London, as shown in Table 6.2, we still welcome the opportunities, as they arise, to sponsor US company issues here. The features we principally look for, in identifying a potentially exciting issue for a US company, may be summarized as follows:

- *Financial record.* The past may only be a reassurance, but it is of critical importance. Any US company coming to the London market should have achieved sustained, consistent and rapid growth over at least a three-year, and preferably a five-year, period to secure the interest of UK investors.
- *Prospects.* There must be strong evidence that earnings growth will continue at a respectable rate for at least the next two years, and preferably beyond. This is obviously the key to a successful issue. We would expect to satisfy ourselves that projections for growth in underlying markets served and/or any expected changes in market share were soundly based.
- *The Board.* The composition of the Board is of critical importance in demonstrating that the company is genuinely ready to cope with the transition from being privately owned, and run exclusively for the benefit of a small group of proprietors, to being publicly owned and committed to taking account of the needs of outside shareholders. A company which has been sufficiently far-sighted to appoint non-executive directors of undoubted standing well in advance of contemplating a public offering can be seen to have faced up to the question of its wider responsibilities, and will thus be given a more enthusiastic reception by potential investors.

   At the very least, we expect one, and preferably two, non-executive directors to be appointed prior to the flotation, who bring to the board experience of other UK listed companies and provide reassurance to UK

Table 6.2: *US companies making an initial public offering in London*

	Market	Share price (pence) at offering	Share price (pence) in April 1987	Current market capitalization (as of April 1987 in £ million)	Historic P/E ratio (exchange rate $1.60:£1.00)
1982					
International Signal & Control	Listed	155	275	469.0	20.7
1983					
Dataserv	Listed	75	178	43.7	19.9
Cobra Emerald Mines	USM	63	65	6.5	–
Chemical Methods Associates	USM	115	18½	2.2	30.0
1984					
Optometrics (US) Ltd	USM	55	23	2.3	–
Process Systems	Listed	92	36	19.3	–
CVD*	USM/Listed	105	–	–	–
Holmes Protection Group	Listed	100	184	113.2	9.0
Great Western Resources	Listed	160	98	39.7	31.4
Petrogen Petroleum	USM	80	23	2.7	–
1985					
Lexicon	Listed	115	33	2.9	–
Colorgen	USM	90	32	3.6	–
Infra Red Associates	USM	94	66	4.4	13.2
Lysander Petroleum	USM	65	31	5.0	–
Pacer Systems	USM	170	175	8.1	20.0
1986					
Borland International	USM	125	140	69.6	19.0
Mrs Fields	USM	140	222	333.0	30.1
Klearfold	Listed	118	108	10.8	12.3
Tribble Harris Li	USM	112	156	19.5	29.4

* Acquired by Morton Thiokol, Inc. for $2.50 per share, valuing the company at $33.9 million.

investors that they will ensure that the interests of outside shareholders are taken seriously in the boardroom.

- *Corporate structure.* UK investors generally prefer a simple structure, with any trading relationship post-flotation between the company being floated and other companies controlled by its directors or major shareholders being kept to a minimum. Again, the presence of non-executive directors will provide reassurance that any such continuing trading is being carried out on an arm's-length basis.
- *Shareholders.* Inevitably, name recognition is of some importance when UK investors are faced with an unfamiliar US investment opportunity. Where the company is a wholly owned subsidiary of a well known US corporation (Hoskyns, for example, a UK company floated by Schroders at the end of 1986, was previously 100% owned by Martin Marietta Corporation), then the UK investment community is more likely to have confidence in state-

ments made by that corporate shareholder in the prospectus as to its intentions for the future. The identities and aspirations of US shareholders outside the Board, particularly if the existing shareholders are to retain the majority of the shares post flotation, clearly constitute a major concern of the sponsor at the time of flotation.

- *Reporting accountants/auditors.* For a US company coming to the London market, it is essential to involve a major accounting firm to act as reporting accountants, and we would usually take the view that it was preferable for the firm involved to have been the company's auditors for a reasonable period prior to flotation. While it is obviously feasible to involve a major accounting firm solely as reporting accountants, and not as auditors, investor confidence in the company benefits from the accountants having been involved for a lengthy period in advance of the flotation. Conversely, a series of changes in auditors over the five-year period prior to flotation inevitably raises questions.

- *Rationale.* It goes without saying that for a successful flotation in London, any US company needs a plausible reason for coming to the London market. If the rationale spelled out in the prospectus relates primarily to future international expansion, it should be capable of credible substantiation: vague statements of future intent to develop overseas not only fail to persuade but may also be positively counter-productive. The London market is moderately receptive to the idea that a US listing is costly both to attain and to service but it is obviously much less comfortable with any suggestion that a higher valuation would be achieved by coming to London or that less disclosure is required. Even if the real reason for coming to London involves the ability to float on the basis of projected earnings rather than historic results (in other words, a higher valuation at that point in time) we would suggest that a company coming to London for that reason should stress that flotation in London simply enables it to accelerate its public offering, for cogent business reasons which can be included in the prospectus.

There is a sense in which new issues always comprise opportunities which can be readily passed up in favour of safer harbours for an investor's money. US issues in the London market have to compete particularly hard to demonstrate management strength and attractive future prospects, partly because of the questions which arise as to why they are coming to London and partly, sadly, because of the track record of so many of the companies which have come this route in the past. Nonetheless, a successful issue by a US company coming to London will of necessity involve the same key elements, referred to above, as any other successful flotation: investors buy stock because they think they will make money doing so. They buy stock at the time of a new issue because they believe they are being let in relatively early on in the company's development and that the company's future growth will be sufficiently rapid to compensate for the fact that investment in relatively small (or young) companies is inevitably more hazardous than investing in large established blue chip companies.

At the time of flotation, people are always acutely sensitive to the questions relating to management (are key executives staying on?), future transactions (will this be the last they ever hear of the company concerned?) and commitment to UK shareholders (will it be a 'float and forget'?). As sponsors we regard it as part of our role to ensure that these questions are addressed up-front.

- *Pre-launch education.* Any US company coming to the London market will have to give great care to the way in which it educates the press, brokers, analysts and investing institutions prior to the launch. Aside from carefully constructed presentations, it may be appropriate to invite selected journalists, analysts and fund managers to spend time with the company on its home territory in the US. The company cannot assume that UK investors will be familiar with it, however well known or excellent it may be in its own territory. As an illustration, it may be the case that those close to the Mrs Fields flotation, which was significantly undersubscribed on flotation, assumed, having spent a great deal of time with the company in the US, that the same degree of enthusiasm could be transmitted three thousand miles away in London; this was not the case. It is interesting to note that as analysts and investors have gained a better understanding of the company, the share price has out-performed the market from the flotation price to the present, even though the share price went to a significant discount immediately after the flotation.

MISCELLANEOUS OTHER ISSUES

In the course of the work involved in bringing about a US company IPO in the London market, there are a number of other issues which almost invariably arise. Some of these can have a bearing on the way in which the issue is received in the London market, and below we set out a brief review of the points involved.

- *US GAAP/UK GAAP.* UK investors are, obviously enough, normally used to analysing companies on the basis of UK Generally Accepted Accounting Practice, and would seek to apply UK GAAP if by doing so the underlying earnings were lower rather than higher. There has, however, generally been an unfavourable reaction to those US companies which have come to the London market with financial statements based on UK GAAP, when US GAAP would have yielded lower earnings. The general rule seems to be that it is safest to use whichever of the two sets of accounting practices gives rise to the lowest earnings figure, and thus the highest applicable price–earnings ratio at any given price.

We would normally advise US companies to stick to US GAAP, whilst including in the accountants' report a reconciliation showing the effect on, for example, the tax charge, goodwill amortization, etc. of applying UK GAAP.

- *Dividends.* Generally speaking, companies which are growing rapidly are expected in the London market to re-invest most of their earnings, in order to fuel continuing expansion without recourse to constant issues of new equity. Nonetheless, it is a feature of the London market that some emphasis is always placed on at least a minimal yield being available from the time of flotation. Investors typically expect that from this admittedly low base, dividends will tend to grow in line with earnings. This is generally somewhat different to normal practice in the United States, where a majority of fast growing companies do not pay dividends, and pay-outs generally are significantly lower than they would be in the UK.

- *Meetings with UK investors.* We do not usually stipulate that the company's by-laws should entrench the undertaking to keep UK investors properly informed about the progress of the company by having all shareholder meetings in the UK. We do, however, always seek from the company the strongest possible commitment to having regular briefings with the analysts and the Press in London whenever a major announcement is issued. In the context of any potentially controversial shareholder-approval being sought, it is obviously preferable for the company to have the relevant meeting of shareholders in London, so that it cannot be accused of failing to give its UK shareholders an opportunity, without undue inconvenience, of coming along to question the company and raise any objections they may have.

- *SEC restrictions.* It has been a regular feature of most issues by US companies in London that the sponsors have sought a US legal opinion to the effect that the issue does not contravene the SEC requirement that the sale of securities to US citizens be registered under the 1933 securities legislation in the US. US lawyers who are in a position to issue such an opinion have gradually become more cautious about the length of time for which it was necessary to restrict US investors from acquiring stock in the company concerned; it now tends to be the case that US investors have to be prevented from acquiring stock issued in London for at least 12 months after the flotation, and for this prohibition to be entrenched in the company's by-laws, legended on the company's stock certificates and incorporated in every document relating to the flotation. The effect of all this is in some ways to lead to an untrue or misleading market in the company's shares for that 12-month period, since a major contingent element amongst the potential investors are precluded from participating. It is to be hoped that in due course, as market standards around the world tend to coincide and investors focus on the underlying investment attributes of companies they are acquiring shares in, irrespective of where they happen to be listed, that the SEC will be prepared to confirm that a somewhat shorter quarantine period is all that is necessary.

CONCLUSION

Selling US companies' stock in the London market always provides a challenge to us as practitioners, and may also provide the London investment community with opportunities to participate in sectors of US business they would not otherwise have considered investing in. As markets develop worldwide, it is to be hoped that the proportion of good quality US companies coming to London rises, since this will ultimately best ensure that current suspicions are dispelled. In the long run, the familiarity of UK investors with the problems of valuing overseas companies, particularly those subject to fluctuating exchange rates, should enable London to continue to increase its share of the international IPO business.

Chapter 7

Equity Entering and Leaving Japan

John O'Donnell

This chapter looks at Japan as a source of equity capital for foreign companies and contrasts this with an explanation of how and why Japanese companies, even with Japan's generally very low domestic interest rates and a high savings rate, have been able to raise equity-related capital abroad, sometimes at more competitive rates than are available at home. In making this comparison, this chapter investigates the character of the Japanese domestic equity market and the ingredients that go to make up that market. It tries to show how and why this market is changing to accommodate the purchase of foreign equity by Japanese investors and what foreign companies should be aware of when listing their shares in Japan.

THE DOMESTIC JAPANESE EQUITY MARKET

Initially, most funding for Japanese companies came from bank loans. It was not until 1968 that there was the first full public offering of shares in Japan. This was an issue arranged by Yamaichi Securities for Nippon Gakki, the world's largest manufacturer of musical instruments. Up until that time, shares were issued at face value. The Nippon Gakki issue was the first issue to obtain the market price. There were, however, no legal restrictions on companies issuing shares at market price. It was merely a matter of custom. While it was easy to encourage companies to issue shares at the higher market level, there was not the same incentive to change dividend policies, which were also based on par value. These dividend policies have stayed the same, resulting in very low dividend yields, with Japanese investors looking instead for capital gains. This structure allowed Japanese companies to plough most of their profits back into the company and go for growth. The situation was acceptable to Japanese investors because there was no, or very limited, capital gains tax in Japan. Moreover, this situation was supported by the very narrow market in companies' shares. On average, only 30% of a company's shares are traded, which has in turn supported the potential appreciation of share prices. The very nature of Japanese companies has more of the attributes of a partnership between management and employees, with shareholders notable by their absence. This situation is reinforced by Japanese employment practices.

This narrow market can be explained by the way in which Japanese companies have historically formed themselves into groups known as Zaibatsus. These were broken up after the war but were largely reconstructed by formal and informal means as soon as the post-war occupation of Japan ended. The structure of these groupings encouraged extensive cross-holdings between companies. Such holdings were as much for relationship reasons as for investment purposes. The prohibition on holding companies in Japan, and the lack of importance, until recently, placed on consolidated accounts, has tended to encourage this type of cross-holding and a business approach in which equity participation is linked to commercial agreements. This has led to the narrow market in companies' shares, contrasting sharply with the prevalent Western form where 100% owned subsidiaries are grouped under the flagship, publicly quoted holding company and where the only meaningful accounts are those that are consolidated. So common are these cross-holdings between Japanese companies that 30–50% of the average corporation's outstanding shares may be simply unavailable at any price. These blocks cannot be traded without rupturing a complex web of business relationships. They are, therefore, only traded with the consent of the company concerned.

The practice of having a substantial portion of a company's equity in firm and friendly hands received a major boost with the 1971 amendment of the Securities and Exchange Act. This amendment set the ground rules for tender offers in the open market and, together with the 1972 Bendix tender offer for part of the equity of Jidosha Kiki, pushed Japanese management into taking protective measures to avoid what was seen as the distinct possibility of a wave of takeovers. The one limit on management's drive to get equity into firm hands is a listing requirement enforced by the Japanese Stock Exchange. This requires a minimum float of shares to be available for trading, thus enabling a fair price to be formed. In practice, this liquidity requirement is not onerous, allowing markets to be narrow and enabling management to achieve a high share price, thus making for easier access to cheap equity capital. Moreover, the very high price/earnings ratios achieved acts as a discouragement to any company hoping to make an acquisition. Japanese investors, adapting to this type of market structure, have tended to be very trading-orientated.

ARE JAPANESE SHARES REALLY OVERVALUED?

Even after 19 October 1987, Japanese companies are quite expensive and should become more so. But Japanese companies, for the most part, do not place a high premium on high rates of earnings and dividend payouts. Rather, they depress earnings and re-invest the funds. They can do this because of their stable shareholder base. There is generally no pressure to push earnings up. While this situation applies to medium- and smaller-size companies, it is changing for the international Japanese company.

Japanese accounting principles allow Japanese companies to understate earnings, thereby reducing their tax burden. There is every reason for them to minimize earnings since Japan's corporation tax is one of the highest in the world, currently 53%. For instance, pharmaceutical companies, which sell drugs directly to doctors and encourage them to buy through offer discounts, can set aside large sums for potential but unquantifiable losses on discounting. For all Japanese corporations, earnings can be minimized because depreciation periods tend to be much shorter than in the US and UK. Thus, when an investor decides to invest in a Japanese company, it is not an instant decision. He has to look at a company's reputation and its formal and informal links. This will involve looking at a company's land holdings, its corporate relationships and its distribution networks. Such networks and relationships are an immensely important part of a company's value and take years to build up, as evidenced today by the frustration of many foreign companies trying to penetrate the Japanese market.

For the following reasons, Japanese companies are, however, not as expensive as they seem:

- The published ratings are on a parent company basis and thus make no allowance for the contribution of subsidiaries, as shown by the following earnings per share comparisons:

	Hitachi	Matsushita Electric	Toyota Motor Corp.
Parent	31.4	50.4	95.7
Consolidated	50.7	92.4	129.6

(The above figures are from the end of the following months: Hitachi, March 1986; Matsushita Electric, November 1986; Toyota Motor Corp., June 1986.)

Domestic investors still rely almost entirely on parent accounts in making profitability and growth judgments. There are now, however, many pressures on Japanese companies to improve disclosure. It is likely that consolidated accounts will become increasingly recognized for the purposes of making investment decisions. This could result in a quite significant re-rating of a number of companies.

- On a net cash flow basis (retained earnings plus depreciation), the rate of investment among Japanese companies is much higher. As of 30 January 1987, the Morgan Stanley Capital International World Index price to cash earnings ratio was 8.4%, while the US was at 8.2%, UK at 8.5%, Japan at 14.2% and Hong Kong at 18.1%. High growth economies should have a higher rate of investment.

- Japanese companies do not re-value their assets. Some assets on the books of Japanese companies are at pre-war levels. On a true asset value basis, companies in the US and UK are selling at about 1.8 times book value, while for Japan it is around 3.5 times as stated. For Japanese companies, however, this is a wholly unrealistic valuation. For many companies, it is estimated that the real figure should be 1 times or even less. At the time of writing, Sumitomo Bank, for instance, had an equity portfolio valued at approximately 50% of the bank's own market value.
- Interest rates in Japan are extremely low. The discount rate is currently 2.5%, with demand bank deposits offering only 0.26%. Earnings yields for Japanese companies, which currently come out at 1.6% on a parent company basis, are not inconsistent with the level of interest rates.

Japanese companies' earnings are currently quite weak. While earnings are depressed, it makes the market look expensive. Japanese shares, however, are more highly valued because the supply and demand situation for equity in Japan is much more favourable. Japanese pension funds, for instance, only have 15% of their funds in equities, compared to 60–70% in the UK and 40% in the US. As Japan's pension funds invest more in equity, there will be even more money chasing fewer shares. Moreover, the Japanese government is probably in favour of the share prices being kept high because such a policy will help its privatization programme. It also makes Japanese companies less vulnerable to takeovers by foreign companies.

INSTITUTIONAL INVESTORS

The category of 'institutional investor' covers a number of types of investor, each of which has different characteristics. Until recently their interest in foreign equity (and, for some, even domestic equity) has been very limited. But with the recent changes that have taken place in the rules under which they operate, institutional investors have the potential to become a major influence in the foreign equity markets. The following details about the size of institutional investor funds are based on the Bank of Japan's asset calculations and definitions.

	Date measured	Yen (trillion)	US$ (billion)
Banks (mainly city banks)	8/86	211.7	1356.9
Corporate investments		n.a.	n.a.
Investment trusts (equity and bonds)	10/86	29.0	179.8
Life insurance companies	9/86	59.6	388.2
Non-life insurance companies	5/86	12.4	91.9
Postal insurance and annuity funds	9/86	30.4	197.7
Special money trusts and fund trusts	9/86	17.2	112.0
Trust banks	8/86	33.3	213.6

(The exchange rate used varied as the relevant statistics became available).

Japanese companies also form a major investing group, but there are no official statistics available. These companies have enormous resources, but they tend to shy away from discussing their investments. According to the Nikkei Press, however, it was estimated for 1986 that Japanese companies put Y30 trillion ($196 billion) into Zaiteku. For 1987, the total is expected to reach Y50 trillion ($327 billion). Zaiteku, which literally means financial engineering, is a vague term for the market arbitrage activities of Japanese companies. Investment in securities is used to supplement traditional corporate income. From a report in the *Nikkei Newsletter* (February 1985), it was estimated that around half of Japan's foreign bond investments in 1984 were accounted for by Japanese companies.

INDIVIDUAL INVESTORS

As of 30 June 1986 (provisional estimate from the Bank of Japan), Japanese individual investors' financial assets totalled Y512.6 trillion ($3.2 trillion). Of that amount, only 11.5% (or $36.4 billion) was invested in domestic equity. Much of individual investors' money is on deposit, currently running at Y321.2 trillion ($1.98 trillion). A change in the tax status of interest earned on certain types of deposits, which would impose withholding tax on such interest, could be introduced in 1988. Such a change could abolish the tax exemption for interest income on small bank deposits and postal savings. This, together with the current very low level of interest rates in Japan, should push more Japanese savings (which continues to accumulate at a rapid rate, see Table 7.1 below) into the Japanese equity market.

Table 7.1: *Personal savings as a percentage of GNP in 1985*

	Savings Ratio (%)	Nominal GNP ($ billion)	Savings ($ billion)
US	4.25	3989.0	169.5
Japan	17.5	1331.0	232.9
W. Germany	11.5	624.6	71.8
UK	12.25	451.7	55.3

Until the mid-1970s, the individual investors' major thrust was into deposits and corporate bonds as companies sought finance for growth. The next stage was a move into government bonds, a result of the deficit financing brought about by the oil crisis. The most recent trend has been a shift both into bank deposits, because of the progressive deregulation of interest rates, and into domestic equities. For a comparison of the relative importance of individual, corporate, institutional, government and foreign shareholdings of Japanese equity, see Table 7.2. Arguably, the next big thrust by domestic individual investors will be into international equities as investors become more sophisticated and because of the imposition of withholding tax on some interest income.

Table 7.2: *Holdings of Japanese equity by type of investor*

	1981	1982	1983	1984	1985
Government and local government	0.2	0.2	0.2	0.2	0.2
All banks (including investment trusts and annuity trusts)	19.2	19.0	19.4	19.9	21.1
Life insurance companies	12.5	12.6	12.7	12.7	12.7
Non-life insurance companies	4.9	4.9	4.8	4.8	4.7
Securities finance companies	0.9	0.8	0.7	0.7	0.7
Other financial institutions	1.4	1.4	1.4	1.5	1.5
Business corporations	26.0	26.3	25.9	25.9	25.6
Securities companies	1.8	1.8	1.9	1.9	2.1
Individuals and others	28.5	27.9	26.7	26.3	25.4
Foreigners	4.6	5.1	6.3	6.1	6.0
Total	100.0	100.0	100.0	100.0	100.0

PURCHASING JAPANESE EQUITY

The stock exchange structure that operates in Japan today was set up in 1949, and was founded on the membership system and modelled along US lines. This was preceded in 1947 by the break-up of the groupings of Japanese companies, which resulted in a massive release of shares, with individual investors substantially increasing their holdings. This event changed the whole character of share ownership in Japan.

The Japanese houses' monopoly over the servicing of investors in Japanese listed stocks began to weaken in January 1982 when those foreign houses with a representative office in Japan had their commission charges reduced to 27% of the standard stock exchange commission rate. In January 1986, six foreign houses became the first foreign members of the Tokyo Stock Exchange. A second attack came in the latter part of 1985, when several houses in the US started to gear themselves up to make net markets in a limited number of highly liquid, and particularly American-orientated, yen equities. This trend, which had been going on for some time in Europe in select Japanese equities, was officially followed in London in October 1986 with the advent of Big Bang.

In Japan itself, the investor is serviced by the securities houses' extensive network of offices and by the limited number of foreign houses. The foreign houses, which are to date almost exclusively located in Tokyo with generally one office each, concentrate mainly on institutional investors. The domestic securities houses' total network of branches number over a thousand, each with their own sales teams. These sales people visit their institutional, corporate and individual clients on a regular basis. Securities houses also service their individual clients by having sales booths in a number of supermarkets.

The unit of trading for Japanese equity is generally a thousand shares, but for very expensive shares the unit is a hundred. There is one exception: Nippon Telegraph and Telephone (NTT), where the trading unit is one share. (The first quotation for NTT shares was Y1.6 million per share.) The breakdown is comparable for foreign shares listed on the Tokyo Stock Exchange (TSE) where the trading unit also starts at a thousand, providing the average closing price is below Y3000. There are, however, four other categories, depending on the price of the shares. All orders are placed through exchange members, with custodian services offered by trust banks, city banks and securities houses. Settlement takes four business days. The administration of trade settlement is very efficient.

THE CHANGING JAPANESE ATTITUDE TO FOREIGN EQUITY

Of the total net capital outflow from Japan in calendar year 1985 of $81.8 billion, some 2.1% net found its way into foreign equity. For 1986, of a total net capital outflow of $132.4 billion, the net percentage accounted for by foreign equity was 5.3%. By the end of 1986, net investment in foreign equity had risen to nearly $2 billion per month. The potential for further growth is considerable, particularly when compared to the funds flowing into the foreign bond markets, as shown by the following figures (in $million) for Japanese net overseas investment:

	1983	1984	1985	1986
Bonds	13 688	30 476	63 493	93 024
Stocks	804	134	1 748	7 048

As a strict legal matter, there are no eligibility requirements covering the public offer and sale of shares in Japan. If, however, foreign shares offered publicly are to be listed on the TSE, the exchange demands that the foreign shares first be listed on a foreign securities exchange designated as an 'Eligibile Foreign Stock Exchange' by the TSE. Even if the foreign shares are not to be listed on the TSE, in order for them to be marketable in Japan, it will be necessary as a practical matter for there to be an established secondary market for the shares outside Japan. It is only securities companies licensed to do business in Japan, including the securities operations of foreign banks, that may underwrite, sell or arrange the distribution of securities, including foreign shares. The definition of a foreign security under Japanese law is narrow and prohibits the sale in Japan of such instruments as depositary receipts and bearer participation certificates, though for some of these instruments the situation may change.

MAJOR PURCHASERS OF FOREIGN EQUITY

To date, it is the individual investor who has been the major purchaser of
foreign equity, accounting for 65–70% of all foreign shares placed in Japan.
Since 1971, there have been no restrictions on how much an individual can put
into foreign equity. Until April 1986, institutional investors were subject to a
limit of 10% of total assets. This 10% limit covered all overseas investments,
including bonds, stocks and property. Such institutions could also have other
regulatory, as well as voluntary, restraints. For example, insurance companies
were authorized to invest in certain securities, including foreign shares, but the
aggregate amount of investment in all stocks, both Japanese and foreign, was
not allowed to exceed 30% of total assets. Their initial overseas investments
were into high-yielding straight debt instruments such as US Treasury bonds,
UK gilts and Eurobonds. The total number of Japanese investors – individual,
corporate and institutional – who invest in foreign equity was estimated to be
around 100 000 as of 5 November 1986. The number of active individual
Japanese shareholders was estimated to be 4.7 million as of 18 July 1986. This
gives a further indication of the market's growth potential. There are a number
of changes that have occurred since 1984, or are expected to occur, which are
helping to turn the purchasing of foreign equity by Japanese investors into a
major growth area:

- The Japanese securities houses began making markets in foreign shares. To
  sell such shares to the individual investor, who was by far the biggest
  purchaser of this kind of security, it was necessary to show that there was a
  liquid market and thus that the investor would not be tied to his investment. This was the key to opening up the market.
- In addition to deepening the secondary market, the listing of foreign shares
  on the TSE has allowed investors access to information printed in Japanese
  about these foreign corporations. There is also the publicity surrounding
  such listings, many of which have been accompanied by a public offering of
  shares. All this has helped to stimulate investor interest in foreign shares.
  The number of foreign companies listed on the TSE went from 11 at the end
  of 1984 to 52 at the end of 1986. A further 50 were expected to list in 1987. In
  Japan, all listed shares are normally dealt with through the stock exchange.
  This situation also applies to foreign shares listed on the TSE. From looking
  at turnover figures, it is obvious that the secondary market is developing
  very quickly. Foreign stock turnover on the TSE, measured in billions of
  yen, was 239.1 in 1983, 186.2 in 1984, 1706.6 in 1985 and 2302.0 in 1986. This
  growth is due, in part, to the potential seen in this area of business by the
  securities houses. For listed shares, there is also a certain obligation on the
  part of the listing agent to maintain a secondary market in Japan.

    Listing foreign shares favours Japanese individual investors because
  such shares can be used for margin trading. Listing also allows investors to

stay in touch with a living market operating in the same timezone as themselves and denominated in yen. Individuals tend to be very trading-orientated, however. For example, as of March 1986, direct individual shareholdings (excluding trusts) accounted for 50% of the domestic shares held in US, 30% in the UK and 25% in Japan. Compare these numbers with the June 1985 figures showing the percentage of turnover accounted for by individual investors, as measured by the number of bargains. In New York, individuals accounted for 28% of the turnover, in London 29% and in Tokyo 41.6%.

Japanese individual investors, on the other hand, should become firmer holders of foreign equity. Because the average dividend yield for the shares of Japanese companies is so low, currently 0.6%, such investment would not normally be attractive to shareholders seeking current income alone. This has reduced the incentive for shareholders seeking current income to own domestic shares and, moreover, has caused them to sell shares quickly for the sake of capital gains rather than hold for income through dividends. The converse should be the case when purchasing foreign equity.

- Tax changes. From 1 January 1986, dividend and interest income from foreign securities was given similar tax treatment to that applicable to domestic Japanese securities. Up until that time, tax treatment was more severe on income from foreign security investments. This change could be complemented by the possible abolition of the tax exemption on interest income from postal savings and small bank deposits, which should push some of these funds into the equity markets.

  Currently an investor is allowed to trade 50 times per year, providing the volume does not exceed 200 000 shares, before he is liable for capital gains tax on such profits. From 1 April 1987, however, the allowable number of trades per annum for this tax exemption was cut to 30 times, providing the volume is not over the reduced figure of 100 000 shares. For investors, there is therefore an incentive to seek the more expensive shares offering the greatest capital gains potential.

- The easing of restrictions on institutions investing abroad. Because the yen was perceived as being too weak against the major currencies, the Japanese authorities were initially very hesitant about lifting the 10% total assets limit which determined how much institutions could invest abroad. Encouraging further capital outflows would have increased the dangers of trade barriers being raised against Japanese exports. With the sharp appreciation of the yen in 1986, however, the authorities raised the ceiling to 25% in April. While this was a substantial increase, it was not as big as it first seemed. Included in the new guidelines were Sushi bonds and foreign currency deposits which were previously excluded and together, on average, accounted for 10% of the assets of such funds. The ceiling was further increased in August 1986 to 30%.

- Foreign shares look attractive when compared to Japanese equity, not withstanding the fact that Japanese companies tend to understate their profits and build up reserves of hidden assets. With the listing on the TSE of foreign companies which pay high dividends, Japanese investors, with comparative information on these foreign companies now available in Japanese, are beginning to look at Japanese shares in terms of the more orthodox return on investment. These shares, with their high price/earnings ratios and very low dividend yields, seem less attractive. This is particularly so with the creeping capital gains tax which Japanese investors are now having to accept. This has major implications for the long term stability of the shareholder base of Japanese companies.

CONCERNS FOR FOREIGN COMPANIES LISTING AND ISSUING IN JAPAN

A considerable number of foreign companies from different geographical areas have now completed a TSE listing, having built up the required shareholder base either through a primary or secondary public offering of shares or through the brokerage route. Their experience has highlighted a number of areas of concern. With proper planning, foreign companies listing in the future should be able to avoid these difficulties.

Timing

It is not possible to submit a listing application until after the annual general meeting (AGM) of shareholders. Thus, the timing of that meeting can be of considerable importance. It takes a minimum of three months for the authorities to process listing applications. This is divided into two months with the TSE and one month with the Ministry of Finance. If the shareholder base is to be built up through a public offering, a further month is required. The filing of the necessary registration documents for a public offering can only be done once the listing application has been processed. A listing on the back of a placing through the brokerage route does not require the extra month necessary for a public offering. This is the tightest schedule. The process's speed very much depends on how many applicants the TSE is handling at a particular time. The preparation of a listing application takes a further four to six weeks, but this can be done prior to the AGM and once the results are announced. It is also required that the actual date of listing falls within the company year following that of the financial statement used in the application.

Pricing

This is another area where problems can arise. The pricing for a primary or secondary public offering is based on the previous day's closing price. If the price drops sharply during the offer period, which lasts some three to four days, it can affect the standing of the company with investors. Some price stabilization may therefore be necessary. In addition, a volatile share price immediately after the listing encourages selling and thus it is also necessary to try and maintain a stable share price at that time. Foreign shares sold through a public offering have been priced at every level from a 3% discount to no discount at all. The normal discount is around 1.5 to 2%. The amount of the discount, if any, depends on market factors such as the market perception of the company, what is going on in the market at that time, how much risk the listing agent/lead manager is willing to take and so on. Timing is thus very important. When using the brokerage route, shares are sold at the market price.

Composition of investors

The composition of investors targeted by a company when listing on the TSE depends on how the company would like to develop its business in Japan. There is generally plenty of flexibility. It is, for example, possible to put greater emphasis on private corporations or banks. To this end, it can be helpful to do a sounding mission so that companies can judge first hand the possible reaction of various categories of Japanese investors. This would also enable the company to get to know the various people in Japan who are helping with the listing and public offering of shares.

Reporting requirements

The TSE requires all applicants to disclose both a consolidated interim balance sheet and a profit and loss statement. These, however, do not have to be audited. If a company publishes only a consolidated profits and loss and an unconsolidated balance sheet, it will be necessary – as a bottom line – to produce an unconsolidated profit and loss so that the two statements are consistent. It is, however, preferable that a consolidated interim balance sheet be prepared.

Acquisitions

The question of acquisitions, and their impact on the timing of a company's application for a listing, is an area that has caused some problems. Initially, the TSE took a very rigid approach. If the acquisition was material, it necessitated a full year's delay before listing. For a Japanese company, the word 'material' was defined to mean acquisitions 1% or more of the acquiring company's size. For foreign companies, a figure of 10% or over was discussed from time to time, but nothing official appeared in writing. The TSE, however, began to change its stance, and this culminated in a new set of guidelines, published at the end of 1986, which required that:

1. If the listing candidate acquires a company which is larger than itself, no application for listing may be made during the company's fiscal year in which the acquisition occurred, or in the following company year. Thus, if the acquisition takes place in company year 1987, then the earliest an application could be filed would be company year 1989.
2. If the listing candidate acquires a company which is 50% to 100% of its own size, an application may be made in the company year following the year of the acquisition, provided that the acquisition occurred in the first half of the year. If the acquisition took place in the second half of the company year, then an application may not take place until the second half of the following company year. In this latter case, the interim statements would form the basis of the application.
3. If the listing candidate acquires a company which is less than 50% of its own size, there are no restrictions.

Acquisitions, for these guidelines, is defined as the sum total of all acquisition made during the company year. The percentage calculation comparison is based on total assets, sales and pre-tax net income. The highest of any of these three comparisons is the factor that will determine the position. In the case of a sale by a company of part of its business, the impact, calculated on the same basis as those for determining the consequences of an acquisition, must not be 50% or more. Otherwise, one company year's delay is necessary after the year in which the divestiture took place. Thus, for a divestiture in company year 1987, the earliest the company could list would be 1989. If, however, the sale is 25% to 50% of its own size, the same rules apply as in (2) above.

SERVICING INVESTORS AFTER LISTING

When servicing Japanese investors after a TSE listing, it must be remembered that the market is completely different from, say, the US where the stock market is dominated by large institutional investors, all of whom demand considerable attention. In Japan, where the majority of investors in foreign equity have up until now tended to be individuals, this kind of service is not expected. British Telecom found that after-listing service in the US was quite demanding and they have had to station an investor relations executive in the

US. But in Japan, the company found this unnecessary, although BP is now considering such an appointment. Foreign companies usually service Japanese investors through regular roadshows and the distribution of the annual report in Japanese. With the high level of flowback that some companies have experienced, however, it seems there is much to be done to condition Japanese investors so that they are comfortable as longer term foreign equity holders.

There has been much concern among Western companies about flowback from the Japanese market. On looking at what has happened recently to those companies that have listed, however, there have even been a limited number of examples where the shareholding after listing has increased as more shares are brought in from outside by Japanese investors. This improving situation should continue because, among other things, institutional investors now have increasing scope to purchase foreign equity and because the amount of funds available in Japan for such investment is growing. All foreign shares listed in Japan that are traded on the TSE must be held in the custodian account

Table 7.3: *Outflow of TSE-listed foreign stock from the pool available for Japanese trading*

Company	Listing date	Form of placement	No. of shares offered (thousands)	No. of shares on first date of record		Balance as of 31 Dec. 1986
Sears Roebuck	6/84	Brokerage	–	114 250	(8/84)	1 662 350
Walt Disney	6/85	,,	–	146 750	(9/85)	551 350*
Security Pacific	9/85	,,	–	526 350	(10/85)	265 900
National Australia Bank	9/85	Primary	10 000	9 256 000	(1/86)	5 035 000
Telefonica	10/85	Secondary	15 000	13 541 000	(12/85)	10 250 000
Philip Morris	10/85	Brokerage	–	321 250	(12/85)	278 940*
3M	10/85	,,	–	172 470	(11/85)	125 540
Dresdner Bank	10/85	Secondary	750	47 900	(5/86)	73 450
American Express	11/85	,,	1 000	378 800	(1/85)	999 000
Bell Canada	11/85	Primary	5 000	279 350	(12/85)	3 191 250
Union Bank of Switzerland	12/85	Secondary	75	38 037	(4/86)	9 224
Cable & Wireless	4/86	Primary	8 000	6 590 000	(7/86)	11 326 000*
Westpac Banking	5/86	,,	25 000	22 967 000	(6/86)	18 030 000
Toronto Dominion Bank	5/86	,,	4 000	3 313 800	(6/86)	2 236 900
Procter & Gamble	5/86	Brokerage	–	250 050	(7/86)	155 550
British Telecom	5/86	Secondary	180 000	76 625 000	(8/86)	72 850 000
McDonald's Corp	7/86	Brokerage	–	1 360 800	(7/86)	1 043 050
Waste Management Inc	7/86	,,	–	677 150	(9/86)	258 100
Barclays Bank plc	8/86	,,	–	1 921 000	(9/86)	1 189 000
Eastman Kodak	8/86	,,	–	658 350	(9/86)	105 050
Canadian Imperial Bank	9/86	,,	–	998 000	(9/86)	906 000
SmithKline Beckman	9/86	,,	–	175 000	(11/86)	122 800
Commerzbank AG	10/86	Secondary	1 000	n/a	(5/87)	535 880
Du Pont	10/86	Brokerage	–	98 050	(11/86)	79 250
Royal Bank of Canada	10/86	,,	–	241 800	(10/86)	174 600
RJR Nabisco Inc	11/86	,,	–	170 150	(11/86)	141 550
BTR plc	12/86	Primary	3 000	n/a	(n/a)	1 908 000
FPL Group Inc	12/86	Secondary	1 000	n/a	(n/a)	824 100
AGA	12/86	,,	1 300	n/a	(n/a)	1 180 000
Volvo	12/86	Brokerage	–	n/a	(n/a)	478 600

* Recent stock split.

of the Japanese Securities Clearing Corporation (JSCC). It is very difficult to get exact figures on flowback because some investors, particularly institutional investors, may prefer to hold their foreign shares in a separate custodian account from the JSCC account. Thus, the outflow of equity from the JSCC is only part of the story and may give the impression of a greater flowback than is actually the case. If, however, shares are taken out of the JSCC's custodian account, it does reduce the liquidity of the Tokyo market (see Table 7.3).

If shares of a foreign TSE listed company are brought outside the TSE, they must be transferred to the JSCC account before they can be sold on the exchange. For a listing, whether the shares are transferred to Japan through a primary or secondary offering or through the brokerage route, they must be put into an account with the JSCC at least four days before the listing. Once it is confirmed with the JSCC that the required number of shares have been transferred to the account, then the TSE receives final approval from the Minister of Finance to go ahead with the listing.

FOREIGN INVESTMENT INTO JAPANESE EQUITY

Foreign investment in Japanese equity started in the 1950s. The first foreign investment in Japanese shares, the purchase of shares in Teijin Ltd, was organized by Yamaichi Securities. Initial purchases were subject to strict conditions. At first, interest in Japanese equity came mainly from the US. The Japanese securities houses began to establish their international network in 1953, with the first overseas office set up in New York. It was not until 1964 that the Big Four Japanese securities houses first established a presence in Europe by opening offices in London. The Japanese authorities limited the number of foreign offices that Japanese securities houses could set up to, in principle, two per year. It therefore took 20 years for the Japanese houses to establish a comprehensive international network.

Foreign investment into Japanese equity or equity-related instruments took many different routes, ranging from direct investment by foreigners into the domestic equity or domestic equity-related market through to the purchase of overseas equity or equity-related offerings. The import of foreign capital into Japan was liberalized in June 1960. This started the first overseas boom in Japanese equities. It also meant that it was now possible for Japanese companies to engage in international financing operations. The first American Depositary Receipt (ADR) issue by a Japanese corporation was undertaken by Sony Corp. in June 1961. It was felt that the issue of ADRs would not only enable foreigners more easily to expand their equity investments in Japan, but would also support the commercial activities of Japanese companies overseas.

The total holding ratio by foreigners in Japanese companies was restricted to 5% or 8%, depending on the particular business sector. This regulatory ratio was gradually raised (with the exception of a certain limited number of

Japanese companies) and has been 100% since May 1976. The restricted list of Japanese companies, the so-called 'designated company rule', was abolished in 1984. Not withstanding a 'free in principle' philosophy towards direct investment by foreigners, the Japanese government retains the option of restricting foreign investments if they are in business sectors identified as 'strategic to the national interest', as defined by the Organization for Economic Cooperation and Development's Code of Liberalization of Capital Movements. In addition, there is a second line of defence by the companies themselves. The percentage that can be held by foreigners is subject to board approval. Most Japanese companies have kept their in-house ratio very low. Sony is an exception, with approximately 40% of its stock held by foreigners.

The issuing of ADRs was suspended in July 1963 following the imposition of the 'interest equalization tax' on US capital exports. This tax substantially reduced the interest of US investors in Japanese equity. Furthermore, the imposition of this tax propelled the growth of the Euromarket, which has become the most important source of international finance for, among others, Japanese corporations. The Japanese stock market boom of 1967/68 saw the real beginning of European investors' interest in Japanese equity. The first European Depositary Receipt was issued in 1964, with several more issued in 1969. In 1973, the US began to phase out the interest equalization tax, and ADRs were once again issued. The history of Japanese depositary receipts followed the fortunes of the domestic equity market, reaching a peak in 1981. They have since lost favour with Japan's issuers for a number of reasons, notably because of the problem of flowback.

The issuing of convertible Eurobonds by Japanese corporations became the next major medium through which to raise international equity-related finance. This was supported by the Japanese stock market boom of the late 1960s and early 1970s. As mentioned before, it was only in 1968 that there was the first real public offering of shares in Japan; this change opened the way for convertible bonds. When raising such equity-related finance in the US capital market, the big problem for Japanese corporations was, as it still is today, the SEC Segmentation of Activities Requirement. The SEC requirement necessitates a breakdown by each geographical area of sales and, more importantly, a net profit breakdown for each division of a company. This, Japanese corporations argue, would allow competitors to discover production costs of their various products and make them vulnerable to competition. In addition to segmentation disclosure requirements, the legal fees for a US issue are approximately twice that of a Euromarket issue. There have, however, been a number of Japanese convertible Eurobond issues, with a US private placement tranche tagged onto them. While the Eurobonds are in bearer form, the US private placement portion still has to be in registered form.

Japanese corporations find, in order of priority, the following overseas markets particularly attractive:

- *The Swiss franc market.* It is particularly easy to issue into this market. No prospectus is required, just underwriting and selling documents. In addition, it is a market that has traditionally had the benefit of very low interest rates and a reasonably stable currency *vis-à-vis* the yen.
- *The Eurodollar market.* By using the swap route, Eurodollar issues, especially warrant issues, can give a more competitive financing cost than the domestic yen market.
- *The Deutschemark (DM) market.* This market offers advantages somewhat similar to those available in the Eurodollar market, but is generally only used when the issuing company needs DMs.

Apart from the flowback problem, depositary receipts (DRs) have lost their attractiveness because of the higher cost of financing when compared to convertible bonds. Shares are issued at a discount (generally 5%), but with convertible bonds the shares are issued at a premium. For a DR, the fees were initially 5% and are currently at 4.5% as against 2.5% for a convertible bond. Issuing DRs means an immediate dilution of equity if this equity represents new shares. For a convertible bond, by contrast, there is no dilution until the bonds are converted and any interest paid can be set off against the profits of the company. With an overseas bond issue, however, there is always the underlying exchange risk until the bonds are converted. Moreover, to issue DRs successfully, it has to be established that the immediate outlook for the company is good. For a convertible bond, the initial year's outlook does not have to be so attractive as long as the following year (and years) look bright.

In the past, Japanese Euro-convertible bonds, particularly those denominated in US dollars and Swiss francs, were popular because of their low cost and more relaxed issuing procedures. Because the secondary market was less developed, however, the bonds tended to be converted very quickly. The shares were sold back to the Japanese market, adversely affecting the share price. With the growth of the domestic convertible bond market, which is now very large and well developed, and with lower interest rates (now only slightly higher than Swiss francs), Japanese issuers – with the exception of Japanese banks – have switched to the domestic market where investors tend to recover their investment by trading the bonds rather than through conversion, as shown by Table 7.4 below.

Table 7.4: *Japanese trading volume* (yen billion)

	Securities outstanding (A) 30/9/86	Trading volume (B) 10/85 to 9/86*	(B) ÷ (A)	Converted/ exercised 10/85 to 9/86
Convertible bonds	5 265	113 720	21.6	550
Warrants	178	578	3.2	nil

* Trading volume figures is for purchase plus sales.

Coupon rates, because of the popularity of domestic convertible issues, are low and, because conversion is slow, issuers have the double advantage of paying a low coupon over a long period and at the same time having limited dilution of the shares. Japanese banks are prohibited under administration guidelines from issuing domestic convertible bonds and thus can only issue in the overseas markets. There are, however, discussions afoot to change this. Japanese convertibles are generally priced very differently from US convertibles. Japanese companies go for a small premium over the closing price (5%), allowing them to obtain a very low coupon. The premium is based on a six-day average price, including the market price on pricing day. The 5% premium is a Ministry of Finance guideline. The Ministry of Finance guideline for a premium on a warrant issue is 2.5%.

WHY USE INTERNATIONAL EQUITY WARRANTS?

The issue of bonds with warrants was made possible by the 1981 change in the Japanese commercial code. Because of the 'Real Demand Rule', it was not possible for Japanese houses to engage in the swap business until April 1984. The abolition of this rule has led to the opening up of the swaps market, allowing Japanese corporations to protect themselves from exchange risks and thus helping to make international equity warrant issues attractive, especially where it gives a lower yen cost than in the domestic market. The swap market opened in June 1984 with a swap-driven issue for Kyushu Electric Power, lead-managed by Yamaichi. It is not possible to predetermine the yen cost for an overseas convertible issue since it cannot be swapped.

There were a great number of Japanese international equity warrant issues in 1986. Under Japan's Securities Industry Autonomous Rules, equity warrants are subject to less restrictions than convertible issues. For example, recurring profit (less tax) necessary before a Japanese company could issue convertible bonds is Y7 per shares. This restriction does not apply to a warrant issue. In the case of a warrant issue, the majority of warrants are not normally exercised until the end of their life. Although it may differ from market to market, there is generally limited initial dilution of the equity and, of course, the company can hedge the exchange risk, thus making this a very attractive method of financing. Overseas convertible bonds, because this market is less developed and the coupons are so low, tend to be converted fairly quickly. Japanese houses have attained a leading position in the lead management of international equity-related issues, aided by the strong participation by Japanese companies in the equity-related Eurobond market (see Table 7.5).

Until recently, Japanese regulations required that the great majority of Japanese companies issuing convertible bonds and equity warrant issues in the domestic market make use of the commission bank system. The commissions that have to be paid under this system are quite high because these banks monitor the financial health of a company and become the guarantor of last

Table 7.5: *Equity-related eurobond issues 1985/86*

Domicile of issuer	Convertibles				Equity warrants			
	1985 no. of issues	$ million	1986 no. of issues	$ million	1985 no. of issues	$ million	1986 no. of issues	$ million
America	12	1282	40	3316	0	0	1	150
Europe	15	1082	13	822	16	1023	51	5502
Japan	43	2519	10	1021	41	1664	144	9801
Total	70	4883	63	5159	57	2687	196	15453
Total Equity Linked		133	10042				253	18140

Source: Yamaichi Securities.

resort, making the required payments to investors in the event of a default. This restricting criteria encouraged many Japanese companies to go abroad for their equity-related financing.

When issuing straight equity, it is much simpler to use the domestic market where the cost is lower compared to an overseas issue of DRs. This is another reason why overseas DR issues have lost their popularity with Japanese issuers. The objective of a DR is not necessarily to attain the lowest issuing cost, however. There could be a niche for this kind of overseas financing for smaller companies with high growth potential which need capital and want to expand the liquidity of their shares in the international market. For this, convertible bonds or equity warrant issues would not be appropriate because such financing would not immediately increase the number of a company's outstanding shares. It is necessary, for some of these companies, to increase the turnover of their shares to attract larger investors. Thus, the issuing of DRs might be an appropriate way to achieve this. The costs, however, will have to come into line with the domestic market to make it attractive.

DOMESTIC VERSUS OVERSEAS EQUITY-RELATED FINANCING

When deciding whether to issue equity-related financing in the domestic market or in the international market, the two most attractive options are currently a domestic convertible bond issue or an overseas equity warrant issue. The domestic market is the natural choice, but the procedure that must be followed is more onerous. This may encourage some issuers to go abroad, especially as they can also treat the offering as a public relations/marketing exercise, updating their international investors on the developments in, and outlook for, their company. The current initial all-in cost (as of February 1987) of a Eurodollar equity warrant issue with a five-year maturity is, in principle, less than 2%. For domestic convertibles, with maturities ranging from six to 15 years, the all-in cost is in the range of 2.2 to 3.5% depending on maturity, rating, trading volume and recurring profit less tax per share, throwing the maturity advantage very much on the side of the domestic convertible.

With the decline in Japanese interest rates, the volume of domestic convertibles has shown considerable growth over the last three years. The number of Japanese companies permitted to issue unsecured bonds in the domestic market is expected to rise from the current 180 to approximately 330 as a result of regulatory changes in April 1987. To issue domestic convertible bonds, companies will now need net assets of at least Y20 billion (previously Y33 billion) or have an A rating from one of the established rating agencies. As of December 1986, there were 545 outstanding convertible issues listed on the Tokyo Stock Exchange. This compares with 30 domestic equity warrant issues. These equity warrant issues are divided into those where the warrants are not detachable and those where the warrants are detachable and can be traded separately.

The first Japanese warrant issue appeared in December 1981 when the issue of warrants first became possible under a revision of the Commercial Code. This revision allowed only non-detachable warrants to be issued in the domestic market while both non-detachable and detachable issues could be sold overseas. The non-detachable warrant issues come in two categories, one where the investor has to pay additional money for the new shares when exercising the warrants and the other type where the investor simply redeems the bonds and uses the cash to purchase the shares. This latter type is very similar to a convertible bond. A domestic warrant issue, however, has to meet the same strict criteria as a straight domestic bond issue, making it more attractive to issue domestic convertibles. In addition, the convertible's cost is lower. Detachable warrants have only been permitted in Japan since November 1985. For these reasons, the secondary warrant market is still underdeveloped. To separate the domestic from the overseas warrant market, detached warrants issued overseas (including detachable cum-warrants) could not be sold in Japan until 1 January 1986. All these international equity-related issues, combined with the roadshows by issuing companies, the stream of foreign analysts visiting companies in Japan and the phenomenal growth of the Japanese industrial machine, have helped to make many Japanese companies household names with foreign investors.

With the decline in Japanese interest rates and a growing concern about too many equity-related instruments building up in foreign hands that could facilitate takeovers, there seems to be a trend – whether for market or policy reasons (probably a combination of both) – towards encouraging Japanese companies to raise their equity-related financing at home. The easing of credit restrictions and collateral requirements that took effect in April 1987 is strong evidence of this. The Japanese market, however, is now well established with international investors and these investors should go on increasing their interest in the market, irrespective of how much international equity or equity-related financing Japanese companies find it attractive to undertake.

On the other hand, for foreign issuers, yen assets are attractive, and they are expected to become more so with the increasing recognition of the yen. From the Japanese standpoint, however, with Japan's huge cash surpluses and all the deregulation that has been taking place, the scene is set for the next stage in the country's development, which is to establish itself as one of the world's leading investment banking powers. Given the lessons that have been learned from the Third World debt problem and the amount of Japanese money that has already gone into the foreign straight debt market, the time is now right – with the aid of advances in communications technology – for Japanese money to have a major impact on the foreign equity markets. This scenario, if it is correct, should introduce more industrial balance, with Japan having a vested interest in the health and prosperity of many foreign companies.

Chapter 8

Issuing into the United States

Albert F. Lilley

Business corporations around the world are now presented with a growing array of financing alternatives as the internationalization of the securities markets facilitates the flow of capital across national borders. The new appetite and flexibility for financing businesses has been driven by numerous developments, including the knitting together of major trading markets around the world through electronic linkages which provide 24-hour securities trading, the privatization of major European industries, improvements in the clearance and settlement of international securities transactions, the invention of new financial products and techniques for hedging currency risks and the initiatives of investment bankers in marshalling and moving large sums of investment capital on a worldwide basis. Nevertheless, the countries involved in this global market continue to maintain and enforce regulatory frameworks which govern access to their particular capital markets. In the case of the United States, this regulatory framework has been in existence for more than 50 years and has evolved into a web of extraordinary complexity and sophistication. The Securities and Exchange Commission (SEC), which administers the US securities laws, has recognized that these laws can be a barrier to the free flow of capital and has undertaken limited initiatives to accommodate easier access by foreign corporations to the US capital markets. The SEC is currently considering further modifications; but US regulation of the issuance, distribution and trading in securities continues to be a significant hurdle for any non-US corporation seeking to tap the US capital markets. This chapter provides a general review of the law in this area.

There are at least eight separate federal statutes which provide the framework for the federal supervision of both the issuance and distribution of securities and also the operation of the securities industry and the secondary trading markets. These statutes are the subject of continuing judicial and administrative interpretation, so that there is an extensive body of federal law (some of it ambiguous, unclear and inconsistent) applicable to those who seek to participate in the US capital markets. In addition, the various states have their own laws (referred to as Blue Sky laws) designed to protect investors within their borders. This chapter will deal with the requirements of only two of these federal statutes, namely the Securities Act of 1933 (1933 Act), which regulates the issuance and distribution of securities, and the Securities Exchange Act of 1934 (Exchange Act), which regulates the trading of securities. Anyone considering entering the US capital markets must, of course, seek the advice of competent US legal counsel if they are to be well informed about the specific impact of the entire regulatory framework upon their plans.

Before discussing the details of the application of US securities laws to the issuance of equity securities by non-US corporations, it is worth pointing out just how far US law can be stretched to protect the interests of US investors. The potential extraterritorial effect of these laws is usually shocking to those unfamiliar with the applicable court decisions and the attitude of the SEC as the chief enforcer of these laws. In general, the US federal securities laws can be applicable to any transnational securities transaction which involves transportation or communication among 'or between any foreign country and any US state or territory, or the District of Columbia'. In other words, a single telephone call into the US in connection with any aspect of a securities offering can be the basis for the application of US securities laws, assuming certain additional jurisdictional requirements can be satisfied.

Whether there will be an attempt to apply US securities laws to a particular transaction depends upon a number of factors, the most important of which being whether the interests of US investors are involved. Established principles of US law permit extending US securities laws to transactions which take place wholly outside the United States if the transactions give rise to an 'effect' within the United States which involves the interests of US investors. Thus, US courts have asserted subject matter jurisdiction when a fraudulent securities transaction that occurred in another country substantially affected investors or securities markets within the United States. If, however, the foreign person or corporation that allegedly violated the US securities laws cannot be found in the United States, it is usually not possible to proceed against that person or corporation in a US court.

The SEC, the Justice Department and other law enforcement agencies in the United States have established elaborate monitoring facilities for detecting illegal conduct in securities transactions. Such agencies cooperate closely with each other and with law enforcement agencies in other countries in fulfilling their respective missions. Recently negotiated treaties with other countries for the exchange of information have materially enhanced law enforcement agencies' capacities to uncover illegal conduct and pursue violators worldwide. Recently, accords have been reached between (among others) law enforcement agencies in the US and Canada and between those in Japan and the UK. Perhaps most notable is the 1982 SEC accord with Switzerland. This removed the haven of the Swiss secrecy laws for those who violate the anti-fraud provisions of US securities laws. Moreover, non-US corporations that may have engaged in conduct which violates US law and escaped the consequences due to lack of jurisdiction over that corporation by a US court, should anticipate that the SEC will have a long memory if that corporation should in the future ever seek to tap the US capital markets. The SEC is in a position to deny access to the US capital markets to any corporation whose past conduct includes a disregard for US law.

GOING PUBLIC IN THE UNITED STATES

1933 Act

The 1933 Act prohibits the sale, or the offer for sale, of securities without compliance with a registration and disclosure process which is designed to make material facts about the issuer, its business and the securities being offered available to potential US investors. In addition, the 1933 Act prohibits conduct in connection with the issuance and distribution of securities which is deemed to be fraudulent. In certain circumstances, where it has been determined that the formal disclosure process is unnecessary for the protection of investors, there are specific exemptions from compliance with the registration and disclosure process that are available. If an exemption is not available, then any issuer of securities subject to the 1933 Act must file a registration statement (part of which is a prospectus containing disclosure material) with the SEC before offering to sell a security in the United States or to a US person. The prospectus must be delivered to prospective purchasers in connection with the offering, and the securities cannot be sold until after the registration statement filed with the SEC has 'become effective'. The process of preparing the registration statement and responding to the comments of the SEC staff, which customarily reviews the registration statement before allowing it to 'become effective', can be time-consuming and expensive. Failure to comply with these procedures can result in criminal as well as civil penalties.

Preparing the registration statement

There are prescribed forms for use in preparing the registration statement, and the advice of knowledgeable counsel is required to determine which is the correct form and to supervise the preparation of this important document. The prospectus is not only a disclosure document, the completeness and accuracy of which will protect the issuing corporation and its officers and directors from liability under the US securities laws. It is also a 'selling document' whose composition and presentation can affect the success of the financing.

As mentioned above, the SEC has recognized that non-US corporations can have special problems in complying with the US disclosure requirements. In November 1982, the SEC substantially revised its registration and reporting requirements for foreign private issuers. In adopting the changes, the SEC stated that it sought to balance two competing objectives. On the one hand, the SEC sought to protect investors by requiring substantially the same disclosure from US and foreign issuers. On the other hand, the SEC sought to promote the public interest by encouraging foreign issuers to register their securities in the United States by permitting them, under certain circumstances, to meet less stringent disclosure requirements than those required of US issuers. The revised registration requirements introduced three new registration forms (Forms F-1, F-2 and F-3) for use by foreign private issuers. The definition of a 'foreign private issuer' excludes both foreign governments and those issuers who have more than 50% of their outstanding voting securities held of record, directly or indirectly, by residents of the United States and whose business is administered principally in the United States, or has more than 50% of its assets in the US or more than 50% of its executive officers or Board of Directors are US citizens or residents. The SEC, however, tends to view Canadian corporations as being part of an integrated North American marketplace and thus Canadian corporations are not always eligible for the special concessions accorded to other foreign private issuers. Accordingly, there are limitations applicable to Canadian issuers that severely restrict their use of the F Forms.

The F Forms mirror in large measure the counterpart forms for general use (Forms S-1, S-2 and S-3). Both F Forms and S Forms generally require disclosure of information such as the following: (i) a description of the issuer's business and properties; (ii) a description of the security to be issued and the trading market for, and the market price of, the issuer's securities; (iii) information about the issuer's management, including compensation, ownership of the issuer's securities and transactions with the issuer; (iv) management's discussion and analysis of the financial condition and results of operations and liquidity of the issuer; and (v) financial statements, selected financial data and other financial information. Following a December 1982 amendment to the SEC's Regulation S-X which prescribes financial statement requirements, both F Forms and S Forms permit a foreign private issuer's financial statement presentation to be in accordance with foreign accounting principles provided that certain reconciliations are included in the prospectus.

This change in the SEC's traditional insistence upon compliance with US GAAP (generally accepted accounting principles) was in response to the fact that it is often extraordinarily expensive and time-consuming for a foreign private issuer to restate its historical financial statements to comply with US GAAP, and that a restatement can create confusion when the issuer has already published financial statements prepared in accordance with principles applicable in the jurisdiction of its domicile. The required reconciliations, designed to assure disclosure of certain financial information in a format and pursuant to rules considered essential to a fair presentation, can be expensive and time-consuming to prepare and can produce significant changes in financial statement results. The F Forms do reduce the scope of the business and industry information required, especially the segment and geographic area revenue disclosures which, as required by the S Forms, can be difficult for many foreign private issuers whose books are not maintained in a fashion which accommodate such disclosure. Issuers can also be reluctant to disclose such information for competitive reasons. In addition, the F Forms reduce the scope of information with respect to the management of the issuing corporation, such as management's employment background, remuneration and security ownership and disclosure of transactions with management.

While the F Forms do allow some flexibility, it can be worth assuming the burdens of full compliance with the S Forms in order to publish a prospectus that contains the kinds of information, and in the format, which analysts and investors in the US are accustomed to reviewing. In this connection, it is worth noting that in March 1985 the SEC published a concept release soliciting public comment on methods of harmonizing disclosure and distribution practices for multi-national offerings by non-governmental issuers. A number of commentators expressed scepticism about whether the SEC's November 1982 innovations with respect to registration and reporting requirements for foreign private issuers had contributed at all to increasing the internationalization of the capital markets.

Nevertheless, efforts continue in an attempt to develop uniformity in disclosure and format for the offering materials of multinational securities offerings. In July 1986, the 30-nation International Association of Securities Commissions formed multinational committees to accelerate, among other things, the access of foreign issuers, broker dealers and investors to each other's markets. In February 1987, the SEC conducted a roundtable on the Internationalization of the Securities Markets, thus showing its serious intentions to deal with the many regulatory issues which continue to impede the international free flow of capital and securities. These and other efforts should, in due course, result in more uniform disclosure requirements for the issuance of securities in world markets. Of course, the uniformity may come not only from further liberalizations of US requirements but also from the imposition of more exacting requirements, particularly in the area of financial reporting, in continental European countries. The ever increasing sophistication of investors around the world may well lead to uniformly high standards of disclosure from issuers of securities, so that non-US corporations will find it increasingly difficult to compete for capital in all of the world's markets without providing complete and accurate disclosure of the information essential to investor decision-making.

As mentioned above, there are three classes of both the F Forms and the S Forms. The F-1 and S-1 Forms are 'long form' registration statements designed to contain the most detailed information on the securities being offered and the issuer's business, properties and financial condition. In contrast, the Forms F-2, F-3, S-2 and S-3 are 'short form' registration statements which permit liberal incorporation by reference to disclosure information contained in the periodic reports which eligible issuers have previously filed under the Exchange Act. For example, the F-3 or S-3 is used by issuers with a 36-month Exchange Act reporting history who also meet certain float (aggregate market value of shares held by non-affiliates) requirements. An issuer eligible to use F-3 or S-3 can 'get to market' much more quickly than the issuer who must use the F-1 or S-1. Not only is the time required for preparation of the registration statement much shorter, but it is likely that the registration statement on F-3 or S-3 will become effective in a matter of days following its filing with the SEC staff since the staff usually does not review such filings. Initial filings on F-1 or S-1 are almost always reviewed, and one must expect a period of at least a month from the date of filing before the offering becomes effective and the selling of the securities can begin. A first-time foreign private issuer of equity securities in the US will be required to use either the F-1 or the S-1, even though the issuer may be a seasoned public company outside the US.

Exchange Act and Exchange Act reporting

The Exchange Act regulates securities trading in the secondary markets. It imposes a system of periodic reporting which provides investors with a regular flow of information to assist them in appraising traded securities. In addition, the Exchange Act contains comprehensive rules to prohibit fraudulent manipulation and other unfair practices in the trading of all securities, whether registered or not, in the US markets. Any corporation required to register a security under the Exchange Act becomes subject to the full range of disclosure regulations contained in the Exchange Act.

Exchange Act registration is triggered for both domestic and foreign private issuers by either (i) the size of the issuer (total assets exceeding $5 million) and the number of security holders (at least 500 holders of record of a class of equity securities) or by (ii) voluntarily using the US capital markets through causing a class of equity security to be traded in the secondary markets. In the case of foreign private issuers, at least 300 of the 500 security holders mentioned in (i), above, must be US residents to trigger Exchange Act registration. Registration under the Exchange Act is accomplished by filing a registration statement on Form 10 (or in the case of a foreign private issuer the somewhat less demanding Form 20-F) or by registering under the Exchange Act simultaneously with a a 1933 Act registration and using an abbreviated registration process on Form 8-A. The content of the Exchange Act registration statement is similar to that required under the 1933 Act, but the disclosure must be updated periodically. Periodic reports are filed on Forms 8-K, 10-Q and 10-K, except in the case of foreign private issuers as explained below.

The 8-K is a current report filed generally within 15 days after the occurrence of certain reportable events. The Form 10-Q is a quarterly report which is filed for each of the first three quarters of the issuer's fiscal year and is composed primarily of financial statements and related financial data. The Form 10-K is the annual report, and is generally as comprehensive in its coverage as a prospectus. The 10-K thus furnishes investors with comprehensive information on a continuing basis, even when the issuer is not currently making a public offering of securities. The SEC has promulgated Forms 20-F and 6-K as a separate set of reporting forms for foreign private issuers. The Form 20-F is a dual-purpose form that may be used by a foreign private issuer not only for registration under the Exchange Act (in lieu of a Form 10) but also as an annual report (in lieu of a Form 10-K). The Form 6-K, which is used in lieu of the 8-K and the Form 10-Q, includes the 'significant' information which the foreign private issuer is required to make public in the country of its domicile, as well as information filed with any foreign stock exchange and made public by that exchange and any information otherwise distributed to security holders by the issuer. Information which is 'significant' to the issuer under Form 6-K generally mirrors the 'material reportable events' required to be disclosed by Form 8-K and the disclosure of financial information as required by Form 10-Q. After information of this type is made public, a Form 6-K must be promptly filed with the SEC. Consistent with the SEC's views regarding Canadian corporations, there are significant limitations on the use of the Forms 20-F and 6-K by Canadian issuers.

Becoming subject to the Exchange Act

Generally, issuers of securities who voluntarily enter the US capital markets, whether to raise capital or to have their securities traded in the secondary markets, become subject to the Exchange Act. A foreign private issuer is deemed voluntarily to have entered the US capital markets if its securities are either listed on a US national securities exchange or quoted on an automated inter-dealer quotation system in the US, such as NASDAQ. This is so even though the foreign private issuer did not make a public offering in the US and its securities were merely acquired by US persons who made securities purchases outside the US. In addition, every corporation that files a registration statement prior to a public offering in the US must sign a written undertaking that it will comply with the Exchange Act's periodic reporting requirements, even though it may not otherwise become subject to the Exchange Act. A foreign private issuer that meets the size and security holder criteria (including having more than 300 US resident holders of a class of equity security), but whose securities have not been registered under the 1933 Act or are not listed on a US national securities exchange or quoted on a US automated inter-dealer quotation system such as NASDAQ (in other words, one who has not voluntarily entered the US capital markets), has the alternative, in lieu of filing Exchange Act reports, of providing the SEC with copies of information which the issuer furnishes to the public in its own country.

A non-US corporation that expects to raise capital through a US public stock offering at some future date may wish to consider prior voluntary compliance with the Exchange Act. As mentioned above, the short-form registration forms F-3 or S-3 are available only to issuers who have been in compliance with the Exchange Act periodic reporting requirements for at least 36 months. Substantial advantages, particularly in terms of timing and costs of financing, can be had through the use of the short-form registration statements. Moreover, for a non-US corporation whose securities are currently traded only outside the United States, the development of an active secondary market in the United States prior to a public offering in the United States can increase the appetite of US investors and thus improve the prospects for a more fully priced public offering in the United States when that occurs. Secondary trading may heighten visibility generally and perhaps help develop a US consumer market for the foreign corporation's goods or services.

OTHER EXCHANGE ACT REQUIREMENTS

When a non-US corporation's securities become subject to Exchange Act registration, the corporation becomes subject to a number of US requirements and limitations that can increase administrative costs and affect the way the corporation conducts its business and the behaviour of its officers, directors and any stockholder who owns more than 10% of its outstanding shares.

Insider trading provisions

Section 16 of the Exchange Act contains the so-called insider trading provisions, which are designed to prevent principal officers, directors and significant stockholders of corporations whose shares are traded in the United States markets from profiting from insider information. Section 16 applies to trades in any equity security, other than an exempted security, so long as the corporation has at least one class of equity security registered under the Exchange Act. Principal officers, all directors and holders of more than 10% of any class of equity security of any corporation with equity securities registered under the Exchange Act must disgorge to their corporations (for the benefit of all of its stockholders) any profits they may realize on trading in the corporation's equity securities within any six-month period.

The only way to avoid an obligation to disgorge profits under this section is to refrain from any trading which could result in the matching within any six-month period of a purchase and a sale of the same equity security of the corporation out of which a profit could have been derived. It makes no difference that within the six-month period, as a result of other trades, an aggregate loss was realized. The rule is applied in a mechanical fashion, mandating disgorgement even though the trading was not carried on with the benefit of insider information. If a corporation has equity securities registered under the Exchange Act, principal officers, all directors and holders of more than 10% of any class of equity security must file with the SEC (and any stock exchange where the issuers' shares are traded) statements of beneficial ownership and changes in beneficial ownership of equity securities of the corporation, so that the transactions which can give rise to liability are a matter of public record.

There are lawyers in the United States who carefully peruse these records and police compliance by notifying corporations of any matching transactions that they discover. Courts have ruled that such lawyers are entitled to a fee from the corporation when, as a result of such notification, the corporation is forced to obtain the required disgorgement from one of its officers, directors or 10% stockholders. A corporation ignores a notification from such lawyers at its peril, since such lawyers represent minority stockholders of the corporation on whose behalf the lawyer would then commence litigation to compel the corporation to seek disgorgement.

The obligations of Section 16 are applicable even though the purchases and sales of equity securities are conducted entirely outside the United States. The initial report of beneficial ownership on Form 3 is due forthwith upon the corporation's registration under the Exchange Act. Persons who become principal officers, directors or 10% stockholders thereafter must file the Form 3 within ten days after the date upon which they gain that status. The statement of changes in beneficial ownership, made on Form 4, must be filed within ten days after the end of each month in which a change has occurred in the ownership of an equity security. Under applicable rules, the granting, acquisition or disposition (and the exercise) of any presently exercisable put, call, option or other right or obligation (whether or not transferrable) to buy securities from, or to sell securities to, another person or any expiration or cancellation thereof, may be deemed to effect a change in beneficial ownership of the securities to which the right or obligation relates and thus require the filing of a Form 4. In addition, such options or rights themselves may be considered equity securities and their acquisition or disposition may trigger a filing obligation. There are complex rules for determining, among other things, what may constitute an equity security, what constitutes beneficial ownership thereof, and whether the purchase and sale is reportable or exempt.

Corporate disclosure

An overriding objective of the US securities laws is to ensure that all facts and circumstances material to investor decision-making are made available to the marketplace in a timely manner. Under Section 10 of the Exchange Act, so-called insiders, who may include officers, directors and others whose responsibility to a corporation bring them in touch with market-sensitive information, will have liability for trading on market-sensitive information that has not been adequately disclosed to the public. Furthermore, the corporation itself can be deemed to have committed a 'fraud on the market', for which it can be liable in damages to its security holders, for having deliberately, or through gross negligence, failed to make timely disclosure of facts and circumstances deemed material to investor decision-making. Any corporation which becomes subject to the Exchange Act must develop a programme with its counsel for accomplishing the timely public disclosure of material, market-sensitive information.

Reports by 5% beneficial owners

Under Section 13 of the Exchange Act, persons or corporations which acquire beneficial ownership of more than 5% of the outstanding securities of any corporation whose shares are registered under the Exchange Act must, within ten days of such acquisition, file a Schedule 13-D with the SEC and mail a copy of that filing to the corporation and to any stock exchange on which the shares are traded. Legislation currently pending would shorten the ten-day period and otherwise strengthen legislative inhibitions on the secret accumulation of shares.

The Schedule 13-D requires the beneficial owner to disclose information identifying (i) the persons for whom the securities were acquired, (ii) the purposes for which the acquisition was made (such as 'investment' or 'to obtain control'), (iii) the source of funds for the acquisition and (iv) all agreements or understandings which the owner may have with anyone else concerning the securities of the issuing corporation. The purpose of this regulation is to keep the corporation and the marketplace informed regarding a possible change in control of the corporation. The Schedule 13-D must be promptly updated.

Tender offers

Offers to purchase the equity securities of a corporation whose shares are registered under the Exchange Act, whether made by the corporation for its own shares or by a third party, must comply with the tender offer rules if the terms of the offer cause it to be a so-called 'tender offer'. The tender offer rules are designed to assure fairness to existing stockholders in considering an offer to purchase their shares. These rules set forth procedural requirements for, among other things, the timing of an offer, how long the offer must remain open and the mechanics for its acceptance and amendments thereof. The tender offer rules also require a detailed disclosure statement not unlike a registration statement. The tender offer rules, along with certain other anti-fraud provisions in Section 10 of the Exchange Act, also impose limitations on the corporation in connection with the purchase of its own securities, regardless of whether those purchases may take place within or outside the United States.

Proxy rules

A corporation must comply with detailed rules with respect to disclosure and procedure when soliciting proxies for any shareholder action by holders of a class of securities registered under the Exchange Act. The proxy soliciting materials must be pre-filed with the staff of the SEC for review. Within ten days of filing, the staff will inform the corporation as to whether it will have comments. The disclosure requirements vary, depending upon the purpose for which the proxy is solicited. For example, when soliciting proxies for the election of directors, the proxy rules require disclosure of detailed information concerning nominees, their remuneration from all sources and pertinent information with respect to transactions involving the corporation in which nominees have a personal interest. Proxy soliciting materials that concern shareholder approval for acquisitions which meet certain standards of materiality will require detailed financial statement disclosure of the target and prescribed pro forma financial information. Failure to comply with the proxy rules risks injunctive relief brought on by the SEC staff or minority shareholders and consequent delays in accomplishing the desired corporate action.

Foreign Corrupt Practice Act

Section 30-A of the Exchange Act makes it unlawful for a corporation whose equity securities are registered under the Exchange Act to corruptly make, offer or authorize payments to (i) an official of a foreign (non-US) government, (ii) a foreign political party, official or candidate, or (iii) any individual whom the corporation knows or has reason to know will give or offer all or part of the payment to such foreign official or party. Such payments, to be unlawful, must be made with the intent of influencing official action in order to obtain or retain business. Where such payments are criminal offences, the SEC retains investigative jurisdiction. Its enforcement responsibilities include bringing civil actions and referring cases to the Justice Department for criminal prosecution where warranted. The criminal penalties for violating these anti-bribery provisions are particularly severe.

There are at least two additional potentially major impacts upon those non-US corporations which become subject to US securities laws. First, the 1933 Act makes it unlawful for any 'affiliate' of the corporation to make any public sale of any securities of the corporation, such as a sale on an organized securities exchange in the United States, over-the-counter in the US, or possibly in an organized securities exchange outside the US, unless the securities in question are registered under the 1933 Act or sold in accordance with an exemption from registration. An 'affiliate' is, among others, a person who directly or indirectly controls the corporation, either alone or possibly as part of a group. The term 'control' is defined to mean 'the possession, direct or indirect, of the power to direct or cause the direction of the management and policies of a person whether through the ownership of voting securities, by contract, or otherwise'. So long as the corporation is in compliance with the periodic reporting requirements of the Exchange Act, there does exist a limited exemption under Rule 144, which will permit securities owned by the affiliate to be publicly sold through brokers in limited amounts on an unsolicited basis.

A related consequence has to do with equity securities offerings wholly outside the United States subsequent to the time when a non-US corporation establishes a market for its equity securities in the US. Once a non-US corporation has a number of US equity security holders, particularly as a result of having voluntarily tapped the US capital markets, the SEC will become very sensitive to the question of whether equity securities issued and distributed by the corporation wholly outside the US may nevertheless flow back to US security holders because of the appetite of US equity security holders for the corporation's securities. In order to assure compliance with US law a non-US corporation with US security holders may be required either to register under the 1933 Act any equity securities publicly offered outside the US, or to utilize lock-up techniques and other mechanisms designed to cause the offered equity securities to come to rest outside the United States and not flow back to US security holders. A group of US securities lawyers recently made proposals to the SEC staff designed to liberalize requirements in this area. The SEC, in connection with its February 1987 roundtable, indicated that new regulations may soon emerge.

THE PRIVATE PLACEMENT EXEMPTION

The 1933 Act's registration process does not apply to so-called private placements, which are the offer and sale of securities to defined classes of financially sophisticated, wealthy investors.

Liquidity concerns

A foreign private issuer's prospects for raising significant capital in the US through the private placement of equity securities, without in due course having to comply with the 1933 Act registration process, are probably still limited despite an increase in US institutional investor ownership of – and demand for – foreign debt and equity securities. Section 4(2) of the 1933 Act, which provides for the private placement exemption, simply states that the registration process shall not apply to 'transactions by an issuer not involving any public offering'. Thus, an investor purchasing equity securities in a private placement represents that such securities are being purchased 'for investment and not with a view to their resale'. There is no general rule as to how long the private placement purchaser must hold such securities in order to fulfil the 'investment intent' which must exist upon purchase, except that under Rule 144 a non-affiliate of an issuer is generally considered free to dispose of securities purchased for investment following a three-year holding period. The SEC created its Rule 144 'safe harbor' to provide some predictable prospects for liquidity through limited sales of privately placed securities ('restricted securities') into an organized trading market for such securities. In order for Rule 144 to be fully available, the issuer of the securities sold through the private placement exemption must, among other things, be in compliance with the periodic reporting requirements under the Exchange Act. If a US purchaser buys the restricted securities of a foreign private issuer which is not in compliance with the Exchange Act periodic reporting requirements, he has limited certainty as to when and under what circumstances the restricted securities can be disposed of consistent with US securities laws, even though there may be a trading market for the securities outside the US. This factor alone could result in a substantial illiquidity discount when the purchase price of the securities is negotiated at private placement.

Recent pronouncements by the SEC staff, however, strongly suggest that US private placement purchasers of equity securities of a foreign private issuer are free to sell those equity securities into an established secondary trading market outside the US, presumably subject to considerations relating to possible flowback to the US. Experienced legal counsel may be able to suggest arrangements which will enhance the liquidity potential for the US purchaser of a foreign private issuer's equity which has an active trading market outside the US. In considering the prospects for marketing its equity securities in the US by private placement, a foreign private issuer must bear in mind that the major purchasers of securities at private placement are managers of financial institutions such as insurance companies, pension funds and endowment funds, as well as wealthy individuals, who are generally sophisticated and capable of negotiating terms which take into consideration liquidity and other factors which can affect the value of the security.

The private placement purchase agreement

The sale of securities through the private placement exemption is customarily accomplished through transactions in which the terms of the sale are negotiated directly with the private placement purchasers. In order for the 1933 Act private placement exemption to apply, the purchaser must be financially sophisticated. It follows that the purchaser will insist upon receiving information about both the issuer and the securities which is relevant to making an intelligent investment decision. The precise information required and the form of its delivery, written or oral, will depend upon the negotiation. The application of Regulation D (referred to below) may, however, require that the pur-

chaser receive a written document not unlike a prospectus in content. Generally, the terms and conditions of the purchase will be contained in a formal stock
purchase agreement. The stock purchase agreement frequently contains rep-
resentations, warranties and covenants of the issuer. Breaching these
agreements would give rise to legal action for rescission of the purchase and
consequential damages. A foreign private issuer may be obliged to agree by
contract to submit to the jurisdiction of US courts. Usually the stock purchase
agreement will also include provisions addressing the liquidity of the purchased securities, such as calling for their registration under the 1933 Act at
some future time or requiring the issuer to comply with the Exchange Act
reporting requirements and other conditions necessary to permit resale of the
securities under Rule 144 or perhaps calling for redemption at some future
date.

Regulation D

Section 4(2) of the 1933 Act is seemingly straightforward in describing the
private placement exemption as a 'transaction by an issuer not involving any
public offering', but specific applications over the years have created much
uncertainty as to the essentials of a private placement. In 1982, the SEC
adopted a series of rules, together referred to as Regulation D, designed to
provide certainty as to when a transaction will be treated as a private placement. While a transaction that does not strictly comply with Regulation D
could nevertheless be a qualified private placement under Section 4(2), Regulation D provides a 'safe harbor' for compliance.

Regulation D defines three separate types of private placement transactions:
Rule 504 transactions, which cover the offer and sale of securities with an
aggregate offering price of less than $500 000 by an issuer not subject to the
Exchange Act reporting requirements; Rule 505 transactions, which cover the
offer and sale of securities by a corporation, whether or not subject to the
Exchange Act reporting requirements, having an aggregate offering price of
less than $5 million; and Rule 506 transactions, which cover the offer and sale of
securities by any corporation, whether or not subject to the Exchange Act
reporting requirements and without regard to the aggregate offering price. The
amount limitations of Rules 504 and 505 include the aggregate offering price of
all the securities sold in the private placement plus any of the same securities
sold during the 12 months before the start of and during the offering and which
are also sold under Rule 504 or 505 or in certain other circumstances.

In the case of offerings under Rule 505 and 506, the issuer must reasonably
believe that there are no more than 35 'purchasers' of the securities offered by
the issuer. For purposes of Regulation D, an 'accredited investor', which is
discussed more fully below, is deemed not to be a 'purchaser'. All Regulation D
offerings are subject to 'integration' rules, which lump together various sales of
securities as being part of the same offering. All of these sales must meet all of

the terms and conditions of Regulation D. Offers and sales made more than six months before the start of or more than six months after the completion of a Regulation D offering will not be considered part of that Regulation D offering.

A Regulation D offering will normally not be available if the securities are sold by any form of general solicitation or general advertising. Regulation D also requires that the issuer must take reasonable steps to be assured that the purchasers are purchasing for investment and not for resale. In this connection, purchasers must be informed in writing that the securities have not been registered under the 1933 Act and cannot be resold unless they are so registered or unless an exemption is available. A legend to this effect is printed upon the face of the certificate evidencing the securities. In the case of Rule 505 and Rule 506, if the purchasers are not limited to 'accredited investors', the issuer must provide purchasers with prospectus-like information concerning the issuer, its business and the securities being offered. In the case of a foreign private issuer, the information requirements are the same as those for Form 20-F. Obviously, satisfaction of such information requirements is much easier if the foreign private issuer is already a reporting company under the Exchange Act.

In connection with sales of securities under Rule 504, or exclusively to 'accredited investors' under Rule 505 or Rule 506, no written information materials need be furnished to purchasers other than the information that must be provided under the anti-fraud provisions of the securities laws to avoid material misstatements or omissions. Regulation D specifically defines 'accredited investors', limiting this category of purchaser to, among other things, certain kinds of banks, insurance companies, investment companies, employee benefit plans, charitable institutions and individuals who meet certain net worth or income tests. In addition, at a reasonable time prior to the purchase of securities under either Rule 505 or 506, the issuer must give each purchaser the opportunity to ask questions and receive answers concerning the terms and conditions of the offering and to obtain additional information supporting the written offering materials already provided to purchasers. Lastly, compliance with Regulation D requires filing a notice on Form D with the SEC no later than 15 days after the first sale of securities in a private placement qualifying under Regulation D. The notice, among other things, includes an undertaking by the issuer to furnish the SEC with copies of the information furnished by the issuer to any non-accredited investors under Rule 505, should the SEC request this information.

Rule 144

Equity securities sold through a private placement constitute 'restricted securities' and generally cannot be resold without first being the subject of a Registration Statement under the 1933 Act or pursuant to a separate exemption from such registration. Aside from sales of equity securities of a foreign private issuer into an established trading market outside the US, as mentioned above, and the possibility of a subsequent sale to another private placement purchaser (in which case the securities would remain restricted as to resale), the only practical prospect for an exempt sale by a private placement purchaser is pursuant to Rule 144. Under Rule 144, a private placement purchaser must generally hold restricted securities for a period of two years. At any time during the third year, provided that the issuer is in compliance with the Exchange Act periodic reporting requirements, the restricted securities can be sold in customary unsolicited market transactions subject to certain volume limitations. After a three-year holding period, the private placement securities are no longer restricted and may be resold in any amounts in any kind of transaction, regardless of whether the issuer is a reporting company.

AMERICAN DEPOSITARY RECEIPTS

A foreign private issuer may also have its shares traded in the United States through the use of American Depositary Receipts (ADRs). ADRs are negotiable receipts issued by a US bank or trust company (the Depositary) to evidence ownership of securities of a foreign company deposited with the Depositary's office or agent in a foreign country. ADRs are employed rather than the simple importation of ordinary shares for three reasons: (i) services provided by the Depositary, (ii) ease of transferability, and (iii) the avoidance of expenses on the death of the shareholder.

The ADRs, when traded in the US markets, are subject to regulation by the SEC and registration under the US securities laws. The registration requirements will depend on whether the ADR is 'sponsored' or 'unsponsored' by the issuer. Basically, any new foreign issue publicly distributed in the US in ADR form will be 'sponsored'. With a sponsored ADR, the foreign issuer arranges for the issuance of an ADR by an American bank. Unsponsored ADRs, on the other hand, are issued without active participation by the foreign issuer.

Both sponsored and unsponsored ADRs may be registered with only minimal disclosure under the 1933 Act's Form F-6. The underlying deposited securities must, however, also be registered under the 1933 Act, unless an applicable exemption from registration can be found. With unsponsored ADRs, the Depositary will most often avoid 1933 Act registration by relying upon the Section 4(1) exemption. Section 4(1) of the 1933 Act exempts from registration any transaction not involving an issuer, underwriter or dealer. In the case of an unsponsored ADR, the Depositary issuing the ADRs is not deemed to be an issuer, underwriter or dealer. If, however, the foreign private issuer is involved in sponsoring the issuance of ADRs, then the Section 4(1) exemption is not available and such issuer will be subject to the extensive disclosure of the F Forms (as discussed above) and the continuing Exchange Act reporting requirements. In such a case, the foreign issuer may want to consider registering the actual shares in the US and not using an ADR arrangement.

CONCLUSION

The internationalization of the securities markets has now attracted the attention of the regulators to a wide range of issues. As pointed out by the then SEC Chairman John Shad when opening the February 1987 roundtable on the Internationalization of the Securities Markets, the areas of concern range across a broad spectrum, including the balance of trade and payments, the international monetary system and the off-balance sheet obligations of banks such as swaps, as well as the particular interests of the SEC such as the international surveillance of market activity, enforcement, clearance, settlement, and disclosure systems and practices. While a truly global securities market, which operates without regard to national boundaries, will not be realized any time soon, it seems reasonable to expect that there will be incremental changes in the US regulatory system which will encourage foreign issuers to raise capital in the US and trade their securities in US secondary markets.

The SEC staff has already made clear its intention to provide new guidance on the following: (i) whether offers and sales of securities outside the US, even though available to US nationals, need no longer comply with the US registration process; (ii) clarification of the 'coming to rest' requirements in connection with the issuance and distribution of securities outside the US; (iii) the circumstances under which a US private placement purchaser of the securities of a foreign private issuer is free to sell those securities into an organized secondary market existing outside the US; and (iv) the circumstances under which a foreign private issuer becomes subject to Exchange Act reporting requirements. In addition, the SEC staff continues to explore ways to develop a reciprocal approach for the registration of securities which are issued and sold across national borders. The approach contemplated is acceptance by the SEC staff of home country disclosure documents as constituting compliance with US disclosure requirements. The SEC staff has announced that it is now developing a proposal that will provide for such reciprocity with Canada and the UK, noting that these initial proposals for reciprocal registration are likely to apply to world class issuers of investment grade debt securities.

Even though there is focus and movement on facilitating the internationalization of the securities markets, foreign private issuers who seek to sell equity securities into the US cannot expect that the US legal compliance hurdles reviewed in this chapter will be substantially lowered. The SEC staff will, at best, move with some deliberation in relieving foreign private issuers of the compliance burdens which are applicable to domestic issuers. Moreover, while it appears that relief is on the way with respect to world class issuers of investment grade debt securities, this does not portend change in the registration process applicable to foreign private issuers who seek to sell equity securities to US persons.

Chapter 9

Bringing Together Disclosure Requirements

Mitchell S. Dupler

In March 1985, the US Securities and Exchange Commission (SEC) published a request for comments on proposals designed to harmonize disclosure and distribution practices for multinational offerings of securities by issuers in the United States, Canada and the United Kingdom.[1] The SEC proposals were made at a time of growing interest in securities issues offered simultaneously in the United States and other countries. Since the SEC published its request for comments, there have been a number of multinational securities offerings. Extensive comments were submitted on the SEC proposals and the SEC has indicated that it continues to be interested in the area, but no formal action has yet been taken.

This chapter begins by summarizing the SEC's alternative proposals. Then, we consider certain of the comments submitted to the SEC with respect to those proposals. These comments illustrate policy issues which must be considered by regulators and practical questions which will need to be addressed by market participants as the SEC moves towards the harmonization of disclosure requirements.

THE MARCH 1985 SEC CONCEPT RELEASE

The SEC's March 1985 concept release was issued in the context of the growing internationalization of world securities markets. Other chapters in this book address aspects of this trend. The SEC concept release spoke of the large and growing number of issuers which enjoy an active international trading market for their equity securities, citing the published statistic that, as of 1984, some 236 issuers had daily active trading in their equity securities outside their home markets. The Commission also referred to several well publicized simultaneous offerings of securities in the United States and other countries. The SEC mentioned a few examples:

In 1983, two Canadian companies, Alcan Aluminum and Bell Canada Enterprises, each offered equity issues simultaneously in the United States, Canada and

Japan. In 1984, British Telecommunications made an initial public offering of over 3 billion ordinary (common) shares with an equivalent U.S. dollar offering price of $4.5 billion in the United Kingdom, Japan, Canada and the United States. Thus, an international capital market, both in primary offerings and secondary trading, is developing at a rapid pace.

The SEC release expressed the Commission's recognition 'that the lines of demarcation between domestic and international capital markets are becoming more difficult to ascertain'. This trend towards internationalization was attributed by the SEC to the elimination of US investment controls, the advent of floating exchange rates, the relaxation of foreign exchange controls, efforts by corporations and investors to diversify funding and investment sources, the repeal of the US withholding tax on interest paid to foreign holders of the debt instruments of US issuers, overall prosperity in the developed countries and new technology. The SEC was not alone in pointing to this trend. As US Senator William Proxmire wrote to then SEC Chairman John Shad a few months before the release, 'an irreversible trend is underway as a result of telecommunications technology in this information age that will accelerate the trading of stocks and other instruments internationally'.[2] Senator Proxmire urged the SEC to focus its attention on the issues raised by internationalization.

In recent years, the SEC has taken some steps to respond to these changes in the international capital markets. In its 9 October 1986 Interim Progress Report on the Internationalization of the Securities Markets, the Commission explained that it has

> attempted to adjust its disclosure requirements to accommodate foreign issuers because of varying differences among the countries in legal and accounting practices. Separate registration and reporting forms have been adopted, including Form 20-F for registration of securities and annual reports under the Securities Exchange Act of 1934. Foreign issuers eligible to use Form 20-F are exempt from the securities laws' proxy and insider reporting provisions. Some of the other accommodations made in that form include requiring that management remuneration need be reported only on an aggregate group basis and that information on transactions with management need be reported only if such disclosure has already been made pursuant to applicable foreign laws or regulations. Annual reports must be filed, but requirements for other periodic reports are based solely on applicable non-United States laws or stock exchange requirements.[3]

With that history in mind, the SEC proposals were intended to encourage multinational securities offerings by harmonizing the prospectus disclosure standards and the securities distribution systems prevailing in the United States, the United Kingdom and Canada. To this end, the SEC requested comments on two harmonization concepts, which it described as the 'reciprocal approach' and the 'common prospectus approach'.

THE RECIPROCAL APPROACH

The reciprocal approach would require agreement by each of the three countries (and any other countries brought into the system) to adopt rules providing that a securities offering document used by the issuer in its own country would be accepted for offerings in each of the other countries, assuming certain minimum standards are met. The SEC release suggests that it could promulgate the necessary rules to permit a foreign issuer to file a registration statement with the Commission pursuant to the Securities Act of 1933. The Commission explained that such a filing might be limited to 'a facing page, a copy of the offering documents used in its own country and a signature page'. The SEC emphasized in describing the reciprocal approach, however, that the filing of such a registration statement would subject the foreign issuer to the same liability provisions of the US securities laws which apply to US domestic issuers, 'including the absolute liability imposed upon issuers by Section 11 of the Securities Act for false or misleading statements contained in the prospectus'.

The SEC sought comments on many questions relating to this proposal, including its assumption that compliance with such a scheme would be less costly and less time-consuming than the existing system because only the issuer's domicile would be reviewing the offering for compliance with the applicable disclosure standards. Of course, a reciprocal approach would give rise to a less uniform system of disclosure than would be achieved under the common prospectus approach. Direct comparison of financial and corporate information between corporate issuers from different countries would be less feasible under a reciprocal system.

THE COMMON PROSPECTUS APPROACH

The SEC suggested, alternatively, that it might be possible for the United States, the United Kingdom and Canada to agree on disclosure standards for offering documents that could be used in all three countries. The SEC cautioned, however, that if it were to adopt rules authorizing such an approach, it would probably expect that the same liability provisions of the federal securities laws would apply to foreign issuers as apply to domestic issuers. Although the SEC indicated that it would be an advantage to have all participating countries share one standard of disclosure, the Commission recognized, and perhaps understated the case when it said, that 'the major disadvantage to adopting the common prospectus approach over the reciprocal approach appears to be the difficulties associated with reaching an agreement with the participating countries on disclosure standards'.

REACTION TO THE SEC PROPOSAL

The SEC's proposals generated considerable interest, as evidenced by the receipt of some 70 comments from issuers of securities, financial, banking and investment companies and trade associations, accounting firms, lawyers and securities exchanges and regulators. The release did not go unnoticed in Congress. A June 1985 report of the Committee on Energy and Commerce of the US House of Representatives directed the Commission to conduct a study 'of the accelerating internationalization of the securities and currency markets and implications of such internationalization with respect to the United States securities and currency markets' and commended the Commission 'for its foresight in recently soliciting comments on concepts relating to certain issues which should be addressed in the study'. The House Committee referred expressly to the March 1985 concept release.

A significant majority of the comments submitted for the public record endorsed the Commission's proposals, but this paper cannot summarize all the comments. Instead, we will focus on issues raised by commentators which are likely to be of ongoing importance as the internationalization of the securities markets continues and efforts to harmonize disclosure requirements proceed. Although many of the commentators expressed the view that agreement on a single harmonized standard for disclosure was an admirable goal, almost all of the commentators recognized that such international agreement would be very difficult to achieve. Many commentators mentioned the difficulties experienced by the European Economic Community in harmonizing regulations and predicted that any effort to agree on uniform standards of disclosure would take many years of difficult negotiations at various levels of government and the private sector.

For some commentators, the most important questions arising with respect to harmonization relate to the procedures and timing for the regulatory review of disclosure documents. Under US practice, a preliminary prospectus (a 'red herring') is prepared and circulated, but comments may be made by the staff of the SEC after the preliminary prospectus is circulated and before the registration statement becomes effective, permitting the securities to be sold. This procedure differs from the practice in the United Kingdom and elsewhere in which there is no customary circulation of a preliminary prospectus. In the UK system, receipt of comments from the SEC staff at the eleventh hour would be substantially disruptive. Although it mentioned the cooperation of the SEC in the Reuters and British Telecom offerings, one American law firm suggested that a general solution to this problem would be for the SEC to adopt a system of 'pre-clearance' in which the Commission staff would offer its comments prior to the distribution of the preliminary prospectus, with the result that 'a preliminary prospectus would in effect be a final prospectus'.[4] No further changes would then be required, except those needed to reflect the determination of the price, developments in the marketing situation or material changes in circumstances between the date of the preliminary prospectus and preparation of the final prospectus.

Alternatively, another American law firm urged that SEC review be completely eliminated for such offerings because of the timing problems it poses. They suggested that 'effectiveness should be automatic within a stated period of time subsequent to filing of a final (pricing) amendment or at a time requested by the issuer and the underwriters prior to such filing'.[5] Such an approach would be a significant departure from standard SEC practice. These suggestions parallel the SEC's recognition that there are important differences between those underwriting methods used in the United Kingdom and elsewhere, and those used in the United States and Canada. Whatever form of disclosure harmonization is ultimately adopted will have to reconcile UK-style announcement and distribution of prospectuses on 'impact day' followed by allotment of securities on 'allotment day' with the US system's focus on the effective date of the registration statement.

The concept release devoted one sentence and a footnote to the possibility that 'inconsistent state blue sky regulations may circumvent the advantages of both approaches'. Each of the fifty states has its own securities laws (blue sky laws) under which domestic and foreign securities must be registered or qualified. The North American Securities Administrators Association, Inc. (NASAA), the association of administrators of those laws, emphasized state requirements and cautioned that 'a major change' in the SEC's disclosure standards and review or in the liability imposed under federal law 'in order to facilitate multinational offerings may require the states, in satisfaction of their obligations under their respective laws, to undertake more extensive review of the quality of disclosure material'.

The NASAA expressed special concerns about provisions of foreign law that might not be disclosed in reciprocal prospectuses, and gave the example of a British Columbia requirement that certain 'corporate acts' be approved by a 75% vote of shares present and voting at a shareholders' meeting – US investors might well not be aware of this rule.[6] The cooperation of state regulators would be vital in any harmonization approach.

Several commentators, including Merrill Lynch Capital Markets, the National Association of Securities Dealers Inc. and the International Advisory Committee of the New York Stock Exchange, addressed the physical arrangements for use of disclosure documents acceptable in other jurisdictions. They urged that the SEC should require that the 'core' prospectus be supplemented by a statement – some sort of wrap-around document. These commentators suggested that a UK issuer coming to the US market could be required to distribute its disclosure document from the United Kingdom together with a statement prepared under US guidelines. The guidelines could require, as one commentator suggested, that such an additional statement summarize the major differences between the two systems of disclosure requirements and could call for a summary reconciliation of the issuer's financial statements to the reviewing country's requirements.[7] One American law firm characterized the contents of such a wrap-around as 'boilerplate' describing differences in disclosure requirements,[8] while others contemplated a much more individual and substantive document.

Commentators were also concerned about the effect of establishing different standards of disclosure for different categories of offerings or offerors. For example, the US Financial Accounting Standards Board expressed its concern that '[t]he adoption of either approach could have significant ramifications on the disclosure standards for domestic issuers in the United States. While changes in current disclosure requirements could be made applicable only to securities offerings by multinational companies, less stringent standards could be perceived as inequities to domestic registrants'. Other commentators were concerned that different standards could lead to issuers shopping around for the least stringent form of disclosure.

Some commentators expressed concerns that, if harmonization was not adopted, US investors and US securities markets could ultimately be deprived of participation in the growing international development of equity offerings. Several commentators were concerned that action by the United States may be needed to avoid being left behind in these developments. Some have urged that Japan be included in any effort towards harmonization, and it has been suggested that applicable Japanese requirements are closer to US rules than are UK requirements. Which jurisdictions should be included in any harmonization will, of course, be subject to debate as it is formulated, but it appears that the SEC is focusing on Canada and the UK.

Mere agreement on harmonized disclosure statements without agreement on the extent of issuers' liability may not be enough, particularly from the perspective of market participants outside the United States. The SEC emphasized in the release that it did not contemplate revision of the US liability standards applicable to foreign issuers under either of the proposed alternatives. The Commission did, however, recognize that the United States experiences a much greater number of civil lawsuits based on securities violations than one sees in other jurisdictions. Non-US commentators emphasized the differences in liability standards and the relative litigiousness of US persons.[9]

SEC DEVELOPMENTS SINCE THE CONCEPT RELEASE

As has been emphasized in other chapters of this book, since March 1985 we have seen a number of multinational offerings of securities. There have been offerings in the United States and other markets in which separate prospectuses have been used, as in issues by Black & Decker, Transamerica and Commercial Credit Company. There also have been offerings, such as those by KLM and UAL Inc., in which a single prospectus has been used in both the US and the 'Euro' offerings. As some commentators have suggested, it is possible that developments in the market will ultimately lead to the equivalent of common standards for 'global' prospectuses, driven by issuers' considerations of economy and efficiency in satisfying regulatory schemes.

The SEC has recently indicated that it is actively considering formal action on its proposal. In a speech on 12 January 1987, then SEC Chairman Shad stated:

> The SEC is considering permitting so called 'world class' corporations to do public offerings of investment grade debt in the US and participating countries, under prospectuses which comply with such companies' domestic requirements, subject to certain minimum provisions. A similar approach is being considered for certain international rights and exchange offerings.[10]

On 17 February 1987, the SEC held a roundtable on developments relating to the internationalization of securities markets. The staff said in its briefing memorandum that a 'reciprocal approach without any reconciliation to US disclosure requirements, under which offering documents accepted in the home jurisdiction could be used in the United States for British and Canadian issuers is being explored for offerings of investment grade debt by world class issuers, and certain exchange and rights offerings'.

It is, of course, impossible to predict with confidence if or when the SEC may take action in this area. The matter is, however, clearly on the Commission's agenda for action. The issues discussed above will have to be addressed in developing any approach to harmonizing disclosure requirements. Among the vital questions for regulators and market participants will be: What procedures for staff review will be followed? How will state 'blue sky' requirements be addressed? What physical form will the documents take? What liability rules should apply? And what jurisdictions will be included? At the same time, the SEC will have to come to grips with the rapidly evolving market practices discussed elsewhere in this book.

Notes

1   50 Fed. Reg. 9281 (7 Mar. 1985).
2   Letter of 23 Oct. 1984 from Senator William Proxmire to SEC Chairman John S. R. Shad.
3   The SEC's Interim Progress Report, submitted to the House Committee on Energy and Commerce, went on to explain: Financial statements for foreign issuers are not required to be prepared in accordance with Generally Accepted Accounting Principles (GAAP) or the Commission's Regulation S-X, provided that a reconciliation of significant variations from those standards is furnished. There are two types of reconciliation. Item 17 of Form 20-F requires a reconciliation only of the differences in the measurement items, i.e. the income statement and balance sheet amounts. Item 18 requires a full reconciliation, including all supplemental data required by US GAAP and Regulation S-X, e.g. full industry segment and geographic data. For most new issues, the Item 18 reconciliations would be required.

4   Letter of 15 July 1985 from Samuel F. Pryor, III, of Davis Polk & Wardwell.
5   Letter of 12 July 1985 from Weil, Gotshal & Manges.
6   Among other matters which the NASAA mentioned as requiring specific disclosure in offerings of securities of foreign issuers were: director's liability, shareholder democracy, reorganization procedures, bankruptcy laws, common law matters such as the 'business judgment rule' and 'piercing the corporate veil', the extent of any limitations or conditions on the limited liability of the investor, applicable tax laws, applicable securities laws and limitations on foreign ownership.
7   See letter of 15 July 1985 from Nicholas A. Rey (Merrill Lynch Capital Markets); letter of 29 July 1985 from Gordon S. Macklin (National Association of Securities Dealers, Inc.); letter of 15 July 1985 from Robert Roosa (International Advisory Committee of the New York Stock Exchange).
8   Letter of 12 July 1985 from Richard E. Lutringer (Whitman & Ransom).
9   See, for example, a Memorandum by the Standing Committee on Company Law of The Law Society (July 1985) which suggested that '[i]t is illogical in our view therefore to suggest that a foreign issuer be exempt from full US domestic disclosure requirements under the reciprocal approach if he is to be exposed to strict liability for material misstatements and omissions laid down in Section 11 of the Securities Act'. The Issuing Houses Association opposed efforts at harmonization, citing, among other factors, the problems posed by US liability rules and arguing that harmonization tends to increase regulation. Letter of 17 June 1985 from H. R. Hutton. See, also, Weil, Gotshal & Manges letter, cited above.
10 Remarks of SEC Chairman John S. R. Shad to the Garn Institute of Finance (12 Jan. 1987); see, also, remarks of SEC Commissioner Aulana L. Peters to Representatives of the Dutch Financial Community (15 Oct. 1986).

Chapter 10

International Clearing

Mary Ann Callahan

All national clearing systems are directed towards the common goal of settling trades, yet the procedures used in the various markets differ greatly. In some relatively small markets, each trade still involves the individual physical exchange of securities, with each payment processed separately. Higher-volume markets and national market systems generally provide more advanced, automated book-entry systems. In these markets, dealers, and sometimes institutional investors, are integrated into a system of synchronized securities and money movements.

As the volume of trading across national borders expands and international equity investment becomes an established part of investor portfolio strategy, each country's domestic market and clearance system will have increasing interaction with foreign counterparts, and the traditional role of national systems will inevitably change. Some national market systems, unless they factor these international investment trends into their planning, may risk their own obsolescence. Domestic markets are being challenged to position themselves within international networks and to pursue international linkages that will enable them to remain competitive by extending their trading hours, gaining new foreign listings, attracting foreign members and adding new financial instruments. With virtually every major financial centre focused today on ensuring its survival within the evolving world order, the closer markets become linked, the stronger will be their need for efficient, coordinated cross-border settlement systems. As the volume of trading across national borders expands, there is an ever-increasing risk that trading profits may become administrative losses.

Centralized clearing corporations have proven effective in many national markets and in the Eurobond market (see Table 10.1). At best, a clearing corporation should offer the following services:

- Central reporting and validation of primary and secondary market trade data.
- Accounting by an industry-accepted method which calculates each firm's updated securities balance for each issue traded.

Table 10.1: *Domestic dealer-to-dealer settlement services available from/or controlled by industry organizations in key capital markets*

Market	Trade clearance	Custody	Money Settlement	International Representation
USA	NSCC/ISCC	DTC	NSCC/ISCC	ISCC
Japan	JSCC	JSCC	Tokyo Stock Exchange	JSCC
UK	LSE	LSE (via registrars)	LSE	LSE
Euro-markets	Cedel	Cedel – via local depositaries (central clearing corps or banks)	Cedel (via local cash correspondents)	Cedel
	Euro-clear	Euro-clear via local depositaries (central clearing corps or banks)	Euro-clear via Morgan Guaranty Trust Co.	Euro-clear
Germany	7 Kassenvereins (KVS) & Auslands-Kassenverein (AKV)	KVS	7 KVS & AKV	AKV
France	Stock exchange	SICOVAM	Central bank	SICOVAM
Netherlands	Kas Associatie	NECIGEF	NECIGEF	Amsterdam shares system
Italy	Stanza di Compensazione (part of the Bank of Italy)	Monte Titoli	Bank of Italy	Monte Titoli
Spain	Madrid Stock Exchange's NSL	Stock exchange via banks	National Bank	Madrid Stock Exchange
Switzerland	SEGA	SEGA	SEGA	SEGA
Canada	CDS	CDS	CDS	CDS

Acronyms used: NSCC – National Securities Clearing Corporation; ISCC – International Securities Clearing Corporation; DTC – The Depository Trust Company; JSCC – Japan Securities Clearing Corporation, owned by the Tokyo Stock Exchange; LSE – London Stock Exchange; KVS – the seven Kassenvereins, the clearing/depository entities in Germany; AKV – Auslandskassenverein, the German international-oriented clearing organization; SICOVAM – Societe Interprofessionnelle pour la Compensation des Valeurs Mobilières, the French clearing/depository system; SEGA – Schweizerische Effecten-Giro AG, the Swiss clearing/depository system; Monte Titoli – the Italian securities depository; its name literally translated means the Mountain of Shares; Kas Associatie – the Dutch clearing service bureau; NECIGEF – Netherlands Centraal Institut voor Giraal Effectenverkeer, B.V., the Dutch depository; NSL – Nuevo Sistema de Liquidacion, the Spanish settlement system; CDS – The Canadian Depository for Securities Ltd; MCC – Midwest Clearing Corporation; MSTC – Midwest Securities Trust Company.

- Securities delivery and money settlement, thus clearing the account balances on settlement day through an exchange of securities and payment between buyer and seller.
- Centralized, local safekeeping. This enables book-entry movements among dealers, and from dealers to their institutional customers.
- Standardized custody procedures for handling dividends, bond interest payments, proxy votes, rights offerings and, for registered securities, links to transfer agents.

For international trades, the idea of constructing a single global clearing corporation for equities, which every market participant would join, represents only one theoretical solution. In a political context, it is probably the most difficult and sophisticated. Just as a single world currency has so far eluded the foreign exchange market, so it seems that establishing a single global clearing approach is not a realistic, short-term goal for the world's securities markets. Therefore, rather than have a single international clearing corporation, many would favour progress towards global clearing standards through cooperative links among the successful national and Euromarket systems. The major clearing systems associated with both the largest capital markets and the most widely traded securities issues are now slowly beginning this odyssey. In effect, they are developing a global clearing approach based on a decentralized network composed of the important clearing corporations.

Today, settlement links between markets fall into two main categories:

1. *Custody links*, involving isolated and fungible custody relationships between clearing corporations (see Table 10.2).

Table 10.2: *Major international custody links (as of 2/87) among key capital markets*

Share issuer's domicile	Custodian	Users
Japan	JSCC	SICOVAM
		Amsterdam shares
UK	LSE	ISCC
		JSCC
Germany	AKV	Cedel
		Euro-clear
		SICOVAM
		JSCC
Spain	Madrid Stock Exchange	JSCC
		LSE
Canada	CDS	JSCC
US	ISCC via DTC	CDS
		LSE
	MSTC	CDS
		LSE
		SICOVAM
France	SICOVAM	JSCC (inactive)
		Cedel
		Euro-clear

Note: Cedel and Euro-clear are also indirectly linked to, among others, Monte Titoli for Italian shares, SEGA for Swiss shares, DTC for convertible Eurobonds, and NECIGEF for Dutch securities. ISCC will soon provide custody services for members of JSCC and the Stock Exchange of Singapore. For an explanation of acronyms, see Table 10.1.

2. *Full clearing links*, encompassing comprehensive clearance-settlement-custody linkages among clearing corporations (see Table 10.3).

CUSTODY LINKS

Custody links are most important for the local trading of foreign securities. For example, if a foreign issuer seeks to list its shares on the New York Stock Exchange, American Stock Exchange or on the NASDAQ (National Association of Securities Dealers Automated Quotations) system, or if its shares are

Table 10.3: *Major international clearing links (as of 2/87) among key capital markets*

Share issuer's domicile	Clearing organization	Users
US	ISCC	CDS
		LSE
	MCC	CDS
		LSE
Germany	AKV	Cedel
		Euro-clear
		ISCC via Cedel
UK	LSE	ISCC

Note: The ISCC/Cedel/AKV link is planned for early 1988. For an explanation of acronyms, see Table 10.1.

purchased for a mutual fund, custody generally remains overseas. The traditional approach was to create a derivative instrument such as a depositary receipt or a mutual fund, although obviously the reasons for having mutual funds goes beyond just custody considerations.

First used in 1927, the American Depositary Receipt (ADR) is the oldest and most common means of handling the foreign stock holdings of American investors. Some 365 foreign issues are now traded on the New York and American stock exchanges or through NASDAQ. In addition, 350 issues are traded over-the-counter and are only quoted in the daily 'pink sheets'. In all, there are over 500 actively traded ADRs, representing the most highly capitalized companies and the most liquid foreign stocks.

American banks issue ADRs as registered substitute certificates representing foreign (usually bearer) shares. These shares are deposited in the bank's overseas branch located in the particular corporate issuer's country of origin. ADRs are either sponsored or unsponsored. With a sponsored ADR, the foreign company sponsors the instrument itself, bears the full costs of issuance, and generally registers the ADR with the Securities and Exchange Commission (SEC). The foreign company is obligated to provide regular financial reporting to the ADR holders. With the tacit authorization of the underlying company, banks create unsponsored ADRs in response to market demand. Although an ADR can be exchanged for the actual shares, this is rarely done.

ADRs trade as US domestic instruments in their own right. Secondary market purchases and sales of ADRs in the US are cleared through the National Securities Clearing Corporation. They are also eligible for custody at The Depository Trust Company (DTC), and for the various other services within the US national clearance and settlement system. Similarly, International and Continental Depositary Receipts, which are issued in bearer form in the Euro-markets, can be traded on many European stock exchanges and are eligible for clearing by Cedel and Euro-clear.

In the US, if a depositary receipt is registered with the SEC, its holders have the same advantages as other beneficial owners of the underlying foreign shares, including eligibility for self-registered voting rights and stock dividends. The ADR holder receives cash dividends in dollars. The overseas branch or custodian collects the dividend in foreign currency, pays the foreign withholding tax and then credits the US depositary bank, which carries out the conversion in order to pay the ADR holder. When paying income tax, US investors can deduct any withholding taxes paid on ADR issues, providing the issuer's country of origin has a double-taxation treaty with the US.

Although convenient, ADRs involve multiple intermediaries which charge fees for custody, currency conversion of dividends and delivery charges. In addition, these intermediaries pass along the generally higher commissions, transaction fees and tax levies of foreign markets. For dealers, ADRs represent an indirect and seemingly costly link to foreign securities. There is some risk in the dependence on the depositary bank and its overseas branch, a greater chance of fragmented pricing and illiquidity and some inconvenience in needing to deal with a particular bank for each issue. ADRs seem increasingly outmoded and unnecessary today, given the viability of clearance and custody links among the generally non-profit-oriented national clearing organizations. Creation of an additional certificate, albeit held within DTC, seems less sensible today than in the past.

A more progressive form of custody relationship provides for local custody without the creation of additional certificates. In 1980, the Amsterdam Stock Exchange introduced the American Shares Amsterdam System, so named because it was initially developed for American shares traded there. (It has since been renamed the Amsterdam Shares Accounting System.) Now Amsterdam-listed securities of other countries, notably Japan and the UK, are included in the programme. In a sense, the Amsterdam Stock Exchange is providing a service for foreign securities in its local market similar to that offered by an ADR bank in the United States. In other words, Amsterdam arranges for the shares to be held overseas, and for currency-conversions of price, dividends and rights. While this system does not create extra paper certificates, the shares are still not fungible with ordinary domestic US, UK and Japanese shares. Rather, the shares are registered under a specific nominee only connected with the Amsterdam programme. As a result, direct book-entry clearance is possible only with counterparties from the Amsterdam Stock Exchange. There are, however, benefits from having these custody positions administered by the regulated marketplace itself; as such, they generally involve fewer fees and are paperless. Custody links of this type seem preferable to the depositary receipt.

Even better is a custody arrangement in which two central depositaries establish a legal basis for using each other's custodial procedures for safekeeping foreign securities. This limited link provides safekeeping functions and usually book-entry deposit/delivery capabilities, although with no automatic clearance function *per se*. When a member of a domestic depositary wants to settle a foreign securities 'sell' trade with a member of an overseas depositary, the domestic depositary can facilitate that settlement by depositing the shares into its account at the foreign depositary for subsequent delivery to the foreign dealer. This centralized deposit/delivery system is used by the Japanese Securities Clearing Corporation (JSCC) for its members' shareholdings in Telefonica, the Spanish telecommunications company traded on both the Madrid and Tokyo stock exchanges. At the Madrid Stock Exchange, the Telefonica shareholdings of JSCC members are held fungibly with those of Spanish brokers.

FULL CLEARING LINKS

Full clearing links can be differentiated between direct links and layered links. Layered links are more complex, involving several clearing corporations. With direct links, such as the relationship linking the International Securities Clearing Corporation (ISCC) and its members to the London Stock Exchange's settlement division, there are actually several sponsors. First, the London Stock Exchange (LSE) sponsors ISCC, a wholly owned subsidiary of the National Securities Clearing Corporation. While not a member firm of the London exchange itself, ISCC sponsors and guarantees the performance of its participants who trade British securities and want to clear them within the British settlement system, Talisman.

In the direct linkage, dealers' trades in the foreign market are cleared in accordance with rules prevailing in the foreign market. Although the clearing organizations are ultimately liable for their members' settlements, their respective members deal directly with each other throughout the clearance cycle. Each member settles with its own clearing/depositary organization and, in turn, the two sponsoring organizations settle with each other. In this linkage, the two sponsoring clearing/depositary organizations act only as conduits for their members' interactions on a day-to-day basis, so each member must be familiar with the procedures and schedules of the foreign jurisdiction.

For example, in ISCC's link to the London Stock Exchange, the ISCC participant in the United States which has traded UK securities over-the-counter with a London member or another ISCC participant reports the trade to ISCC using the LSE's 'bargain record'. Information is provided concerning price, counterparty, settlement date and so on – the usual details any clearing system needs to know in order to process a trade. Transfer instructions are also entered for each trade. ISCC batches together the trade data from all participants and then sends it to the LSE's checking system. The checking system attempts to match the purchase and sale bargain records submitted by LSE firms and by ISCC. For each user, including the ISCC participants, the LSE checking system issues daily reports showing which of its trades have matched and which have not. If a trade is not matched at first, ISCC participants can correct or cancel their input by following the same procedure used by LSE members. ISCC participants can always submit their input and receive their output locally in the US.

Matched trades are next routed to the LSE's Talisman settlement accounting system. Preparations begin for the eventual settlement of securities and funds, generally on the fortnightly account day. Daily reports from Talisman detail the status of completed and pending settlement activity. Several days before account day, in order to receive settlement funds promptly, selling firms must deposit the securities they have sold for delivery through Talisman. ISCC participants' shares are usually held overseas, so they generally arrange to have their UK custodians make the deposits. Then, Talisman continues with its usual procedure, temporarily transferring those deposited securities into its book-entry nominee, Sepon. On account day, Talisman allocates the Sepon securities to buying firms, on a trade-for-trade basis. Talisman automatically notifies the registrar to transfer the shares from the Sepon nominee into the purchasers' names.

While their newly purchased shares are being re-registered, ISCC participants, like LSE members, can arrange delivery-versus-payment to institutional customers by temporarily using Talisman Stock Notes. Eventually, most ISCC participants' UK securities are immobilized in a London custody account or delivered to a third-party institutional client. In all cases, though, the goal is to keep the securities certificates in a controlled environment within the City of London. Money settlement also occurs in London each day, in tandem with the securities movements. Each morning, ISCC pays or receives two net figures, one in British pounds sterling and the other in US dollars, representing the total value of all participants' settlements. In turn, ISCC's bank in London debits or credits participants' sterling and dollar bank accounts.

Even when the foreign members of the foreign clearing entity are not allowed direct access to the local market, a correspondent clearing link is possible. Correspondent clearing links allow cross-border trades to be cleared according to the procedures and time schedules of the issue's most important trading market. For instance, when Canadian brokers sponsored by the Canadian Depositary for Securities (CDS) Ltd trade American stocks with US brokers, their trades are confirmed through the correspondent clearing service available at National Securities Clearing Corporation (NSCC). Settlement of those confirmed trades occurs automatically through NSCC's clearance system, known as Continuous Net Settlement. This clearance system delivers net positions by means of book-entry accounting at the Depositary Trust Company, where NSCC, the US broker, and the CDS member all have fungible custody accounts.

A layered clearing arrangement among multiple clearing organizations requires additional coordination. For participants, however, this provides a more direct 'one-account settlement' system. Foreign clearing corporations do not necessarily know every trader using the international market. In such instances, a gateway clearing corporation can provide the strongest support for intermarket trading. The gateway clearing organization shares responsibility with the individual clearing corporation for the settling of foreign securities positions with the foreign clearing corporation concerned. A good example is Cedel's role as a gateway clearing corporation, working with ISCC and the Auslandskassenverein (AKV) in Germany. Through Cedel, ISCC will soon be able to provide its participants with access to the German clearing system for German equities and domestic bonds. ISCC participants will be able to clear their trades in German securities with all German and non-German members of Cedel, as well as with all members of the AKV, including those who are not direct members of Cedel.

Some of the benefits achieved through this type of link relate to the differences between foreign and global equities trading. Foreign equities are essentially local securities that are traded by foreigners, while global equities have worldwide funding sources and multiple secondary-market listings. An international network can help link the domestic and Euromarket systems, bringing foreign equities into the international realm. Linking domestic markets into an international network also provides a means of influencing the operation of the manual clearance methods used in some markets. The cost of integrating these manual procedures into the automated environment is constantly being lowered by the growing availability of low-cost technology, which can be economical even on a small scale.

Full links among clearing corporations represent the most practical and most promising step towards developing an internationally-harmonious equity clearing system. Collaboration among central clearing corporations seems to be the most productive way to navigate the channels between the world's financial centres. Each organization has an in-depth knowledge of the dealers it represents, and is uniquely familiar with the special features and requirements of local financial instruments. These national corporations can fairly represent their own constituencies' international needs and commitments. The collective expertise of a network of effective clearing corporations will make it possible to maximize efficiencies and gain new benefits from the industry's past investment in clearing systems and thereby avoid 'reinventing the wheel'. This collaboration by clearing corporations promises to create a global network greater than the sum of its parts.

FOR FURTHER INFORMATION

Brochures and documents about the clearing linkages cited in this chapter are generally available from the clearing corporations mentioned. In addition, the works of several other key organizations are strongly recommended. For a comprehensive summary of trading, clearance and custody practices in some 23 major capital markets, consult the two-volume *ISSA Handbook*, published by the International Society of Securities Administrators (c/o ISSA Secretariat, Union Bank of Switzerland, att. WLGB/WLSO, P.O. Box 645, 8021, Zurich,

Switzerland). The latest edition was published in February 1987. For information on technical standardization within the international securities industry, contact the International Standards Organization (ISO), headquartered in Geneva, Switzerland. ISO Sub-Committee 4 (Securities) has proposed a number of standard formats for securities transactions, an international securities numbering system and related standards.

Chapter 11

International Investor Relations

Jerome Hanan

In January 1986, the New Jersey-based Engelhard Corp. convened a forum in Zurich for international analysts. Included were leading industrial analysts from all over Europe, from Banque Bruxelles and James Capel, from Fuji Bank and Nomura Securities, from Merrill Lynch and Smith Barney. The forum's timing was important. Most of the annual European pilgrimages by American companies are concentrated in the spring and summer months. In those months, investors are saturated by invitations. Many presentations are so slick and large that they are more attuned to a marketing drive than a sensible meeting of minds.

Historically, Engelhard's global expansion receives much support from its international investor relations (IR) programme. Though the company is a world leader in the development of performance products based on specialized chemical and metallurgical technologies, this area is little known in Europe where only a few companies are active in the business. The analysts' forum provided an opportunity to educate further the European financial community. The forum's participants were limited to the leading analysts in the field. The analysts were able to share their views about the industry generally, and compare notes and research on the industrial sector in which Engelhard operates. They were also able to confront areas of concern, such as the doubts they had about the company's ability to balance a decline in one operational area – due to the collapse in oil prices – with expansion elsewhere.

A year later the benefits were still evident. Engelhard redesigned its annual report. The management's philosophy was emphasized in the opening section, followed by the directors' report and then several pages highlighting the forum. The chief financial officer's statement was edited to stress the areas most probed by the analysts. The annual report was then mailed to all the company's contacts throughout Europe and the United States. The feedback was positive. Other analysts asked to be included in the next seminar. Many requested a visit to the company's headquarters. Engelhard's shares became more widely traded and accepted. It proved an added bonus that those analysts attending the forum were senior executives. When fund managers now want research material, they can talk to people with a personal knowledge of Engelhard. And because these people are senior executives, any recommendation to buy the company's stock carries much more weight.

At one time, public relations was the blanket label that covered all forms of relations between the corporation and the outside. But this label is no longer accurate or truly relevant. Investor relations is now a sophisticated way of enhancing a corporate image – a reality – of how a company and its management is perceived. The importance of international investor relations (IR) is best illustrated by the existence of consultancies like my own and the functions they serve for their clients. Among my company's clients are Anheuser-Busch, Occidental Petroleum, Greyhound Corp., Goodyear Tire & Rubber, General Development Corp., International Paper, Bowater, Morgan Grenfell and Engelhard Corp. Though these are only a few of the leading companies that apply international IR services today, the list accurately reflects the broad spectrum of companies that now appreciate the value of this activity.

It is hardly surprising that the subtle craft of IR should have originated and first gained acceptance in the United States, the driving force of the world's economy. The global expansion of leading American corporations and the interdependence of the Western industrial nations has led, naturally, to the internationalization of investor relations activity. The partnership between US companies and European investors partly evolved from the increasing use made of the Euro-markets, particularly Eurobonds, by major US corporations. More than 250 US corporations regularly raise money in these markets. This, in turn, has been followed by the widespread listing on European stock markets, opening the door to large scale direct investment in the American economy.

The feedback process now benefits companies of all sizes. For example, General Development Corp., a community and land development company based in Florida, has successfully mounted a fund raising exercise in Europe, using personal and selective meetings, and leaving behind a comprehensive video highlighting both their activities and their executive team. New technology is playing a major role in international IR, with increasing use made of innovations such as satellite conferences between European shareholders and American management. It is a myth that European investors have to be wined and dined at exclusive restaurants. They like IR to be handled in a direct and time-efficient manner. Massive expenditure is not a prerequisite for success.

According to some IR experts, the importance attached to quarterly reports and the performance pressure on US fund managers has led to an unhealthy pressure for short-term gains. Senior executives often voice concern about the damage this causes to companies trying to plan their medium and long term strategy. To a large extent, these pressures are less prevalent in Europe. The vast majority of fund managers in Europe – particularly insurance companies and pension fund managers – are more concerned with stable, long-term performance than many of their counterparts in America. This has led to a keen interest in management philosophy and the support of a stable executive team able to implement a strategy of organic growth supported by related acquisition programmes.

A European IR programme can lead to increased loyalty and support for management. European investors tend to take a longer term view, a fact that is becoming increasingly appreciated in both Europe and America. Given the current takeover activity and the plethora of new methods for financing a takeover bid, the vulnerability of management has increased. In some instances, the loyalty of European investors can prove invaluable.

Contrary to current perceptions, European investors are very interested in companies on the cutting edge of new technology, at least partly because many of these high tech activities are outside the realms of European industry. It is highly unusual in Europe for major investing institutions to abandon a company when the company goes through a lean period or when a takeover emerges. In 1986, the management of Woolworth in Britain was able to fight off a £2 billion takeover from a smaller rival because the 40 institutions that owned 80% of the stock supported a management team that had quadrupled the value of their original investment over the previous five years. This loyalty means that management is supported during short-term hiccups in earnings. Capital is also available during rationalization programmes. These investors are prepared to wait for better times. This kind of support from investors also requires commitment by the company, though IR does not have to be a large drain on executive time or administrative budgets.

The best way to start the process is with a survey. Who will be most attracted by the stock? How well known is the company? What will potential investors want to know? Does past and present performance fit the criteria of institutional investors and if so, whom? The survey allows a target audience to be identified. The list may include research analysts, brokerage salesmen, money managers, investment consultants, pension funds, insurance companies, unit trust groups and regional brokers.

There are three primary objectives to any international IR programme. Firstly, the programme will aim to heighten and sustain awareness of the company in the financial, investment and corporate communities of Europe. Secondly, the programme will seek to supplement and complement the company's domestic IR and corporate communications programme. Finally, the programme will aim to maintain, expand or increase the shareholdings of European institutional investors.

To accomplish these objectives, international IR counsellors have to assume responsibility for financial investor relations and financial and shareholder communications. In addition, international IR counsellors should arrange financial and corporate advertising; if this is not possible, then the IR counsellor should be included as a consultant to insure a common approach.

Past and present contacts in the European institutional, financial and corporate communities are fed into a centralized databank. This facilitates a systematic programme of controlled information release, including all the usual reports. If a marketing director works in harmony with such a programme, the benefits are tangible. A conduit for expansion is created.

The meetings with the investment community can now take place. The financial community is aware of the company and a perception is born. Once this has happened, a media plan is instigated that ensures that corporate highlights receive due attention at least four times a year in the leading financial publications of Switzerland, West Germany, Britain, France and Holland. The media often check out their stories with precisely those analysts and fund managers which the company has already contacted. These analysts and fund managers will have a knowledge of the company, and may be sympathetic to it.

A listing on a foreign stock exchange is sometimes seen as purely cosmetic, but such listings do serve two valuable purposes. Local disclosure requirements provide a sense of security to investors. More importantly, a listing maintains a corporate presence in the local financial press. Media space is a competitive area and a listing often provides the local interest factor, a useful peg on which a journalist can hang a good story. This is a particular benefit when promoting executive visibility.

Management visibility is very important to European investors. They will often identify a company by its senior executives. Investors then study how well this team has performed, analysing the usual criteria of earnings, profits and related ratios within the context of the company's industrial sector, external pressures and competition. Both fund managers and analysts will want to meet senior management and know if they have some form of equity stake in the company, perceived by investors as a powerful motivating force. The team that investors want to meet are the chief executive officer, the chief financial officer and the corporate treasurer. The IR director and consultant should also be present. Investors and analysts want to meet the person with whom they will have the most dealings and see if he has access to the top corporate officers.

Knowledge of a management's philosophy enables managers and analysts to gauge where the company sees itself in the world marketplace over the coming years. This helps them to work out broad parameters by which to judge cash flow, acquisition policy and fund raising, including any stock placement. If an IR programme is conducted effectively, with the right kind of communication, then the investor will be confident that there will be no unpleasant surprises when he reads through his daily financial newspaper.

Regional brokers can be important to overseas investors and their advisers. On the Continent and in the Far East, most analysts are generalists. It is only recently that analysts in Britain have begun specializing in foreign companies and industrial sectors. As a result, many investors will seek in-depth research from small or medium-sized regional brokers who are known to be aggressively expanding their foreign contacts. In many cases, this will be a prerequisite for an investment decision. Personal contact is crucial. A fund manager will talk in far more depth to a trusted analyst or IR consultant than he will to a salesman from a brokerage firm. Whilst a regional broker may get a request for a research report from some apparently obscure mid-European bank, remember that this apparently obscure bank could be managing a very large portfolio. Companies need to know what regional brokers are saying about them and whether it is right or not.

Equally, it is critical to a company that they have an IR representative within the geographic area where funds have been raised. An IR consultant acts as an extension of the company's corporate communications office. As a result, it is usually necessary for an executive team to put aside only a week or so each year for international IR. During this week, a highly organized series of presentations is arranged on a very selective basis in the major financial centres.

European and Far East corporations are now following the American lead, a reflection of the success of international IR. In 1985 and 1986, Nomura Securities and Nikko Securities between them brought over 150 major Japanese companies to Europe for introductory meetings. The meetings were not only aimed at countering the out-dated, negative image of Japan abroad, but also to prepare for the expansion of Japanese companies' manufacturing facilities in Europe, necessary because of the massive currency appreciation of the yen. Conversely, European companies are now moving towards greater direct involvement in the Pacific Basin. In both the Japanese and European cases, international IR has a strategic role to play. It can facilitate companies by countering negativity, opening up opportunities and providing a foundation of local support.

International IR thus facilitates the cross-fertilization of economic activity in two main ways. Firstly, IR can help a company to broaden its share ownership. In the past eight years, Britain's insurance firms and pension funds alone have invested around £40 billion in foreign equities. These are institutions for whom long-term investment in stocks is far more desirable than short-term gambles. Their support during an attempted takeover can make life far less traumatic. A foreign shareholder base can, in turn, make it much easier to raise other forms of finance abroad.

Secondly, IR can help support the marketing of products and services, as well as any general business expansion abroad, including acquisitions and joint ventures. It's not just the much-publicized Japanese car and television factories that are opening in Europe. In 1986 five major Japanese construction and civil engineering firms established subsidiaries in London. These firms immediately entered into joint ventures with local firms. Expansion in foreign markets can be made much easier if a shareholder base is established in the host company. Around 18% of the British Telecom and British Gas issues, together worth £10 billion, were placed in Japan and North America. Any future business expansion into these regions will now be much easier, an indication of just how integral international investor relations has become to the interdependent world economy.

Chapter 12

Twenty-Four Hour Trading

Gordon S. Macklin

The emerging 24-hour global equities market is better called 'the continuous marketplace'. This marketplace will make it possible to complete a deal, somewhere in the world, at any time of day. The continuous marketplace does not mean that securities traders have to be at their desks, in shifts, for the whole 24 hours. It means, rather, that electronic market information systems are continuously feeding each other price and trade data, so that when the traders are at their desks, they can make informed decisions based on accurate and timely information. In the global market, automated systems will bridge the gaps between market hours and time zones, until these distinctions practically cease to exist.

A good example of such a development is the new London Bridge, the automated link between the London Stock Exchange's SEAQ (Stock Exchange Automated Quotations) system and the NASDAQ (National Association of Securities Dealers Automated Quotations) system in the United States. This link, put in place on 22 April 1986, provides the first intercontinental exchange of quotations. At 4 a.m. in Trumbull, Connecticut, the NASDAQ computers begin to receive live price information on some 300 securities traded in London, where it is 9 a.m. American traders, arriving at their desks at 8 a.m. New York time have access to the continuously updated, actual prices from London's competing dealers through their NASDAQ terminals. Similarly, prices on another 300 securities being quoted by NASDAQ dealers are received by the SEAQ computers until 6.30 p.m. New York time, 11.30 p.m. in London. London traders, also starting work at 8 a.m., have through their TOPIC screens the prices with which NASDAQ closed the previous day. During the hours of overlap, when both markets are open and traders are at their desks in both time zones, SEAQ and NASDAQ and the information they exchange permit investors to choose the best markets for their deals. Through nearly 18 continuous hours, the automated systems keep time zones and traders in instantaneous touch with each other.

THE FORCES DRIVING THE GLOBAL MARKET

The development of the continuous global equity market and its automation is being driven by individual and institutional investors, by issuers of securities and by the securities industry. Investors everywhere are searching for promising opportunities in the securities of companies located throughout the world. And well they might. For the period 1975–85, in terms of US dollars, the Japanese stock market was up 373%, the French 324%, the NASDAQ market 319%, Canada 257%, Germany 246%, the UK 237% – and the Standard & Poor's Composite for the US up only 134%. In addition to looking for stock market performances, investors are diversifying their holdings among different countries, economies and currencies. Even to be effectively invested in a major industry, large investors must diversify internationally. An investor in the automobile industry, for example, needs to have positions in Japan and Europe as well as in the US, and an investor in the electronics industry also needs to be in all these three areas.

The global equity market is also developing because many corporate issuers are scouring the world for the least expensive capital. Today, when raising debt capital, most issuers automatically compare structures, rates, size and costs in financial centres around the world, and the same process has started in the equity markets. Hans-Joerg Rudloff, the deputy chairman of Credit Suisse First Boston, has gone so far as to say: 'Today, any company that does not search for capital worldwide is likely guilty of negligence'. By reaching into the entire pool of equity capital worldwide, issuers ultimately assure themselves of a better offering price and broader shareholder base.

In view of investor and issuer demand, securities firms are competing for the new international business. US firms have over 250 branches in 30 foreign countries (excluding Canada and Mexico), while some 150 foreign firms have established branches in the US. Already, 15 to 20 global securities firms operate their own worldwide communications and distribution networks. Their average capitalization is $2 billion; among them, the four top Japanese firms together in 1985 equalled the total profits of all New York Stock Exchange (NYSE) member firms. Medium-sized firms, with $200 million or more in capital, are also active internationally. They are forming cross-border partnerships in order to be able to compete. Furthermore, some 5000 smaller firms, speciality boutiques or regional in their operations, are finding profitable niches in the world market.

Seeing these developments, the equity markets of the world are responding. Linkages between national markets are being forged. Private vendor organizations are speeding the international flow of market information. More efficient and less costly methods of clearance and settlement of international trades are being developed. The response is coming not so much from the traditional exchanges with their single specialist systems ensconced in marble halls. It is coming from the new, automated markets, where the trading is done over the computer by multiple competing market makers, or dealers. Padraic Fallon, the managing director of London's *Euromoney* Publications, puts it this way: 'Of course, it's been known for many years that the notion of a single, expensively vaulted forum for traders would eventually be rendered obsolete by the new [automation] technology. But it has taken the emergence of the NASDAQ system to demonstrate how different and how liquid a computerized over-the-counter stock exchange can be.'

THE NASDAQ EXAMPLE

Through its automated system, the NASDAQ market has a trading floor that runs from Maine to California, from Canada to Mexico. It is 3000 miles long and 2000 miles wide. This trading floor is populated by more than 500 competing market making firms operating from 650 locations throughout the United States. Of these market making firms, 60% are headquartered in cities other than New York. Modern communications facilities tie all these market makers together. The Central Computer Complex in Connecticut and the complete back-up facility for it at the NASD Operations Center in Rockville, Maryland, are linked by 80 000 miles of leased telephone lines to the nearly 3000 cathode-ray terminals in the offices of market makers, financial institutions and regulatory bodies. The computers are also interfaced with the computers of market data vendor organizations, which transmit NASDAQ quotation and transaction information to 150 000 desktop terminals of salesmen and others in the US and in 36 foreign countries. Further, the computers are connected to the computers of the press wire services, and that is how the NASDAQ stock tables get into the morning newspapers.

In terms of dollar volume, NASDAQ is the second-largest market in the US and the third-largest in the world, exceeded only by the New York and Tokyo stock exchanges. Though currently smaller in trading volume than the NYSE, NASDAQ is the preeminent US market for American Depositary Receipts (ADRs) and foreign securities. In 1985, the ADRs and foreign securities on NASDAQ accounted for 1.4 billion shares, or nearly 7% of the total share volume – more than the entire NASDAQ volume in 1974. Dollar volume amounted to nearly $12.5 billion, more than 5% of the total. In 1986, the share volume in 87 ADRs and 173 foreign securities was over 2.4 billion, about 8.5% of the total volume and a 70% increase over 1985. The 1986 dollar volume in these securities was over $25 billion, almost 7% of the total and double what it was in 1985. Thus, the role of non-US securities in the NASDAQ market is growing in both relative and absolute terms.

Indeed, six foreign securities made it into NASDAQ's list of the 50 most active stocks, and Jaguar cars was the third most active of all NASDAQ securities. The ten foreign share volume leaders in our market included securities from the UK, South Africa, The Netherlands, Sweden, Canada and Japan.

All told, the foreign securities on NASDAQ came from 27 countries. All this supports what was said earlier, namely that US investors are seeking global diversification. It also supports the observation that issuers are searching the world for capital, and particularly through the NASDAQ market in the US.

Just as US investor interest in foreign securities on NASDAQ is growing, so is the interest of overseas investors in NASDAQ securities. A measure of this is the increase, overseas, in the number of quotation terminals receiving price and volume information on NASDAQ securities and data on the performance of the market as a whole. In 1984, some 10 000 overseas terminals were receiving this data. In 1985, the number jumped to nearly 14 600. At the end of 1986, it had risen to 20 000. This is a 100% increase in only two years. Evidently, overseas investors are seeking diversification into American securities just as US investors are diversifying into foreign securities.

Of particular interest to investors are the 2700 securities traded in the NASDAQ National Market System (NASDAQ/NMS) with real-time trade reporting. Every trade is reported within 90 seconds, so that the 3000 NASDAQ terminals and the 150 000 quotation terminals leased by market data vendors continually display last-sale and cumulative volume data, as well as bid and asked quotations, on these securities. NASDAQ/NMS companies had average shareholders' equity of $71 million, revenues of $147 million, net income of $6.5 million, a market value of total shares outstanding of $122 million and an average of 9.2 market makers each. Institutional interest in these securities is high – and growing rapidly. At the end of 1979, US and non-US financial institutions held $20 billion worth of NASDAQ securities, or 14.2% of their total market value. By the end of 1986, institutions held $102 billion worth, which was 32% of aggregate NASDAQ/NMS market value.

A UK institution, Ivory & Sime in Edinburgh, exemplifies the interest in American stocks. Ivory & Sime has about $4 billion of equity investments under management. More than half of that is invested in US companies. Of Ivory & Sime's US investments, about $1 billion is committed to NASDAQ companies. Ivory & Sime is not alone. According to a study by Technimetrics, Inc., 82% of European and 55% of Far Eastern money managers responding to its survey invest in US companies with market values like those of the average NASDAQ/NMS company.

All told, 2725 financial institutions had positions in some 2400 of the 2600 NASDAQ/NMS stocks. Their positions totalled better than 52 000, with aggregate holdings of 4.4 billion shares. This brings the average institutional position to 85 000 shares. Of the 2725 institutions, 2145 were in the US and 580, or more than 20% of them, were located overseas. The five countries with the largest numbers of institutions participating in the NASDAQ market are Canada (240 institutions), United Kingdom (175), France (70), Switzerland (26) and West Germany (25). Financial institutions in other countries in Europe, the Middle East and the Pacific Basin also hold NASDAQ securities. Institutions, like individuals, are diversifying around the globe.

INTERNATIONAL AUTOMATION

The rise of automated dealer markets, as illustrated by NASDAQ, is becoming an international phenomenon. On 27 October 1986, the day of the 'Big Bang', the London Stock Exchange restructured itself along NASDAQ lines, with a computerized quotation system, SEAQ, and a competing multiple market maker system. To quote Padraic Fallon again: 'Today, the trading floor of the Stock Exchange in Throgmorton Street is a deserted, echoing chamber, a monument to yesterday. The traders have moved upstairs' – to their computer screens in their own offices.

'Big Bang' reinforces the NASDAQ–London exchange of quotations, which will grow to include many more securities of international interest. More such intermarket linkages, and on a larger scale, will follow. Private vendor organizations will play a major part in getting price information from the various markets and dealers to the end users – the world securities firms and their customers. A worldwide dealer price quotation network will be the first technological building block of the global equity market.

As the quotation network grows, actual trading information will follow. NASDAQ was originally only a quotation information system. Today it receives and transmits last-sale information as well. The same development may be expected to follow in linked international markets. The utilization of the global network for the execution of transactions will develop also – but more slowly. If the domestic experience of NASDAQ with its automatic Small Order Execution System is any guide, firms will prefer to execute orders by telephone until their volume of business and the economics of it dictate otherwise.

In the clearance and settlement area, international linkages can be expected to develop more rapidly. Clearance and settlement represents such a large part of securities firms' trading costs that the firms are putting pressure on the markets to bring those costs down. The newly-formed International Securities Clearing Corporation in New York has already established a working arrangement with London's Talisman clearing organization, and will develop relationships with many other clearing entities. A worldwide network of clearance and settlement arrangements is on the way. The international clearance and settlement network necessarily involves the establishment of rules and procedures in such areas as:

- eligibility standards for participating firms
- eligibility standards for securities
- trade reporting and confirmation
- settlement at multiple depositaries and
- currency exchange rules

The requirements of the clearance and settlement process will help to create much of the regulatory framework for the world equities market.

International automation is going beyond the equity markets. In May 1986, the NASD signed an agreement with the Association of International Bond Dealers to assist the AIBD in the automation of the $2.5 trillion Eurobond market, the largest market in the world after the market for US Treasury securities. Using the expertise it acquired in the operation of the NASDAQ System, the NASD submitted a concept document to the AIBD at the end of July and the design document at the end of September. Since then, it has been working on a request for a proposal that the AIBD intends to issue as a basis for receiving bids to build its automated Eurobond trading system.

THE GLOBAL DEALER MARKET

The structure of the coming continuous global market is emerging quite clearly. There are two chief systems for trading equities: the single specialist system of the traditional stock exchanges, and the competitive multiple market maker system which is utilized by the London Stock Exchange and by NASDAQ. Under the multiple market maker system, anywhere from two to 40 dealers make competing markets in a stock. The average NASDAQ security, for example, has more than 8 market makers. These market makers are geographically decentralized: the more than 500 firms which make markets in NASDAQ securities are headquartered in 38 states and the District of Columbia. Only the information is centralized, through the NASDAQ computer.

A very valuable function of the competitive multiple market maker system is the sponsorship of securities. Firms make markets in stocks which they believe to have potential for investors, and they recommend these stocks to their customers. This is also an important service to issuers, whose stocks must compete with many other financial products for investor attention. The advantages of the multiple dealer system to a global equity market are just as substantial as they are to national markets. Competing dealers, effectively tied together by modern communications technology, can be widely dispersed. This enables them to be close to the investors for whom they trade and to the companies whose securities they sponsor. A flexible, decentralized trading system is uniquely qualified to bridge the time, space, currency and regulatory differences between many countries. The competitive aspect of the multiple dealer system takes on even greater significance in a global arena. Investors will require securities firms to search more broadly and energetically for opportunities, and issuers will be looking to the firms to search more widely and vigorously for investors.

The securities firms who are participating in the growth of the global market know these facts well. This is why firms from many countries are expanding their dealing facilities around the world. The prospect of an international dealer market is also attractive to the firms themselves. In such a market, many firms can participate as market makers, instead of having to funnel their trades through exchange specialists. The visibility and the business opportunities which this permits can be very valuable. From all these considerations, it is apparent that the continuous global equity market will soon be a reality, and that it will be built around a worldwide network of competing dealers.

Chapter 13

Global Trading of Options and Futures

Jonathan Clements

George Hamilton stares out of his London home, anxiously watching the scene on Hampstead Heath. The investment portfolio seems to have just one weak spot, the 10 000 shares in Genprod, Inc., an American company. The stock may have been a good investment when he bought the shares two years ago, but the next six months look tough for both the company and the US market. The prophets of doom and gloom are predicting a spurt in inflation. A rapid price increase wouldn't just dent the real value of his Genprod shareholding. It could also force up interest rates, making bonds more attractive. Or the inflationary spurt might cause the dollar to plunge, slashing the value of Genprod's dividends when converted into sterling. Moreover, the company itself looks weak and the stock might underperform the market. Sell the stock? Possibly, but that would be stupid if inflation doesn't pick up and the company remains prosperous.

The story is fictitious, but the dilemma is real. Instead of selling the stock, Hamilton could choose to hedge his currency and stock exposure by using options and futures. A futures contract is an obligation to buy or sell the underlying instruments at a future date, while an options contract gives the holder the right to buy or sell. The story of George Hamilton remains fictitious at least partly through necessity. While Hamilton could hedge his currency exposure through the dollar–sterling options and futures contracts that are readily available at the London exchanges, the institutional framework for hedging a foreign stock position is still in its infancy. The global market in options and futures is only now beginning to emerge. Already, however, there are indications as to how the market will develop. But before analysing these developments, we must go back 15 years.

BACKGROUND

The revolution in financial futures and options began in Chicago, in 1972 and 1973. First came the introduction of financial futures by the Chicago Mercantile

Exchange. On 6 May 1972, the Merc launched the first exchange-listed currency future. Just over eleven months later, on 26 April 1973, a four-year research effort by the Chicago Board of Trade finally bore fruit. The Chicago Board Options Exchange both opened its doors and introduced the world to the listed stock option. With these two innovations, the stage was set for the boom in financial futures and options, collectively known as 'hybrid' or 'derivative' instruments.

Experimentation did not end with these first two developments. In the 1970s and 1980s, innovations in options and futures have burst on the financial world with the clattering rapidity of machine gun fire. Some shots have found their target. Others have been wildly wide of the mark. Notable among the successful innovations are currency options and stock index options and futures. The first stock index futures contract, the Value Line Index, was introduced by the Kansas City Board of Trade in February 1982. Other US and foreign exchanges quickly followed Kansas' lead (see Table 13.1). Particularly notable is the Nikkei 225 index, composed of Japanese stocks, which is traded on the Singapore International Monetary Exchange (SIMEX), the first time an index futures

Table 13.1: *Contracts Offered by the Leading Exchanges*

	Currency futures	Currency options	Stock index futures	Stock index options
North American timezone				
American Stock Exchange				★
Chicago Board of Trade			★	
Chicago Board Options Exchange		★		★
Chicago Mercantile Exchange	★	★	★	★
Kansas City Board of Trade			★	
Montreal Exchange		★		★
NASDAQ*				★
New York Cotton Exchange	★			
New York Futures Exchange			★	★
New York Stock Exchange				★
Pacific Stock Exchange				★
Philadelphia Stock Exchange	★	★	★	★
Toronto Futures Exchange	★		★	
Toronto Stock Exchange				★
Vancouver Stock Exchange		★		
European timezone				
European Options Exchange		★		
LIFFE†	★	★	★	
London Stock Exchange		★		★
Pacific timezone				
Hong Kong Futures Exchange			★	
SIMEX**	★		★	
Sydney Futures Exchange	★	★	★	★

* National Association of Securities Dealers Automated Quotations.
† London International Financial Futures Exchange.
** Singapore International Monetary Exchange.

contract has been listed abroad. In 1989, SIMEX's example will probably be followed by other exchanges. The Chicago Mercantile Exchange (CME) plans to introduce the Nikkei 225 and the Chicago Board of Trade (CBOT) intends to trade London's FTSE 100 index.

Similar developments are occurring in the sphere of stock index options. The European Options Exchange, launched on April 1978 under the auspices of the Amsterdam Stock Exchange, started trading the American Stock Exchange's major market index in August 1987. The first stock index option, the hugely successful Standard & Poor's 100 stock index option, was introduced by the Chicago Board Options Exchange (CBOE) in March 1983. Though the CBOE has cornered much of the stock options trading, the world's most successful currency options market is undoubtedly the Philadelphia Stock Exchange, which introduced currency options in December 1982. The Montreal Exchange introduced the world's first listed currency option only weeks before the Philadelphia launch. Montreal, however, has never been a serious threat to Philadelphia's dominance within the North American timezone.

This chapter is mainly concerned with the five instruments mentioned above; currency options, currency futures, stock index options, stock index futures and individual stock options. (There are no individual stock futures.) In addition to various arbitrage and speculative opportunities, these instruments also allow international equity investors to hedge their positions against adverse movements in the foreign exchange and stock markets. To date, the number of companies with a foreign listing remains limited. As a result, there has been little interest in trading stock hybrids in one country based on companies headquartered in another nation. Once this happens (as with stock index futures, mentioned above), however, investors will by implication be able to hedge both their equity and currency exposure in a foreign stock simply by dealing in the foreign-listed stock option or future. Thus, once the FTSE 100 is listed on the CBOT, American investors can hedge both their British stock and currency exposure by buying the contract. This, however, will only work because the contract is going to be traded in dollars. If it was quoted in pounds, an investor would not be hedged against changes in the exchange rate.

While discussion here is limited to the instruments mentioned above, it should be remembered that other markets can be influential and important. Their importance is not limited to their role as alternative investment instruments to stocks. For instance, the 86.61 point fall in the Dow Jones Industrial Average on 11 September 1986 was partly triggered by the slump in the bond market. This influence was most graphically illustrated on the floor of the CME. On 11 September, bond futures traders – once they had bid down the price of bond futures by the daily limit – clambered into the stock index pit and began bidding down the price of the stock index futures. The events of 11 September also show the power of the international bond market. While a 24-hour stock market is only in its infancy, a global bond market does exist, and the effects of economic news are often carried round the world via this market.

THREE TIMEZONES

As with the emerging international stock market, the global market in listed hybrid instruments has developed around three distinct timezones. The North American timezone is the most developed. In terms of the five instruments discussed above, particular exchanges have emerged as major forums for each instrument. The CBOE, for instance, is the major centre for stock index options and individual stock options. Other exchanges, however, continue to challenge the preeminence of the dominant exchanges. The American Stock Exchange, for example, is constantly trying to grab stock option business away from the CBOE. Despite this competition, there is an unmistakable trend towards a single exchange cornering the trading volume for each instrument. Overall, this trend is probably beneficial. Often a futures or options contract suffers from illiquidity, making it difficult to close out a position. The competing contracts of different exchanges only compounds this problem. Moreover, when exchanges offer competing products, it makes the life of options and futures brokers more difficult. They have to decide not only when to buy, but also choose between the various competing contracts. In the end, all but one contract usually withers with indifference, eliminating the choice.

In the European timezone, there are three major exchanges for stock and currency options and futures, the London International Financial Futures Exchange (LIFFE), the European Options Exchange and the London Stock Exchange. All three offer options contracts. LIFFE offers futures as well, but there are suggestions that it could soon face competition from the EOE which may be looking to take a share of the European futures market. Though all of these exchanges began trading hybrids within the last decade, they are already well-established. Competition is likely to increase, however. The French government bond futures market opened in February 1986. Other exchanges are poised to follow the French lead. The emphasis, however, is on bonds, not equities.

While the three main European exchanges have quickly established themselves, the same cannot be said for the Pacific timezone exchanges. This lack of development can partly be blamed on uncertainty. In October 1985, the Tokyo Stock Exchange introduced yen bond futures. The next step, the introduction of a stock futures contract, came in June 1987 with the Osaka Securities Exchange's launch of its Futures 50 contract. Trading volume has so far been disappointing. If and when stock hybrid trading finally gets established in Japan, the Pacific timezones' nascent markets for options and futures will probably be thrown into turmoil.

LINKING EXCHANGES: ATTEMPTS AND ALTERNATIVES

Despite the uncertainty in the Pacific timezone, SIMEX – established in 1984 with the help of the CME – has emerged as the most innovative of the area's exchanges. On 7 September 1984, SIMEX and the CME established a mutual offset system that allows positions taken on one exchange to be closed out on the other. Transferring the tradition of the local trader from Chicago to Singapore has not been easy, and SIMEX's liquidity has developed only slowly. Nonetheless, the Singapore exchange has emerged as a leading exchange in the timezone, reflecting two key elements, an effective international settlement link with the CME and a liquid market. The market's liquidity has benefited from the order flow from Chicago, showing that smaller markets do not necessarily suffer when linked with much more active exchanges. The success of the exchange has also been fuelled by Japanese buy and sell orders. Japanese institutions were legally barred from trading foreign futures contracts until the May 1987 change of heart by Japan's Ministry of Finance, but even before then the law was circumvented through the simple expedient of using foreign subsidiaries.

Two years before SIMEX was established, a similar transcontinental link was put in place. In February 1982, one of the earliest attempts to link hybrid markets was inaugurated when the European Options Exchange and the Montreal Exchange signed an agreement to form the International Options Clearing Corporation (IOCC). The first contract was a fungible gold bullion option. The number of contracts traded through IOCC has since been expanded to include currency options. The number of exchanges involved has also increased. In June 1982, the Vancouver Stock Exchange joined IOCC. The latest addition came in January 1985 with the inclusion of the Sydney Stock Exchange. The four exchanges provide the opportunity to trade for 22 hours each day. The IOCC works via an electronic order book, passed from exchange to exchange, allowing investors to buy an option at one exchange and then later sell it at another. While IOCC provides an international clearing system – an integral part of any attempt to link exchanges – the project remains unsuccessful because of the failure to generate a liquid market.

The Philadelphia and London stock exchanges are now working to establish a link for currency options trading, but the prospects for success here also seem dim. The two exchanges reached an agreement on 17 May 1985, and on that day London began trading Philadelphia's foreign currency options. Though the contracts are exactly the same, there is no arrangement that allows dealers on one exchange to close out trades on the other. London Stock Exchange officials seem reluctant to complete the link, possibly because they are worried that London's market will suffer if linked to Philadelphia's much more active currency options programme, something that could happen because the trading hours of the two exchanges overlap. If the link was fully developed, trading in London would possibly suffer because traders would tend to use Philadelphia's exchange during the hours when both markets are open. The apparent paralysis in the London–Philadelphia link highlights a major problem in the global development of options and futures. Even if a foreign exchange offers an attractive, and sometimes identical, contract, international investor interest will be thwarted unless satisfactory international clearing and settlement links are established.

In addition to links across timezones, exchanges have also been seeking links within their own timezone. LIFFE and the London Stock Exchange, despite recent, inconclusive talks, could eventually merge. One compelling reason for such a merger is the dwindling use of the London Stock Exchange's trading floor. With the introduction of the exchange's automated stock quotation system, most trades are now conducted away from the exchange floor. The London Stock Exchange now plans to stop stock trading on the exchange floor, leaving ample space for several futures trading pits.

Other hybrid exchanges are also seeking closer links with stock exchanges. In November 1986, the CME and the New York Stock Exchange announced that they were considering a trading link between the two exchanges. A month later, the CBOE's members approved a proposal to affiliate with the Cincinnati Stock Exchange. Both agreements reflect the growing belief that derivative instruments based on stocks would benefit if traders have better access to stock trading. The CBOE, for instance, fears that it will lose trading volume to the American Stock Exchange and other exchanges if the US Securities and Exchange Commission pushes ahead with the idea of allowing the side-by-side trading of stock options and their underlying shares. Prior to the agreement with Cincinnati, the CBOE had no facility for members to trade stocks.

But seeking links is not the only method that exchanges are using to improve their attractiveness to investors and grab a greater share of the options and futures market. Philadelphia started evening trading in September 1987, and the CBOE has discussed the idea. In November 1986, the Chicago Board of Trade asked the Commodity Futures Trading Commission for permission to trade any of its contracts around the clock. While CBOT officials do not envisage keeping the exchange open 24 hours a day, that possibility throws a whole new light on how international options and futures trading may evolve. Rather than link three exchanges in three timezones to establish a 24-hour market, a single exchange could trade round the clock, with orders directed to the exchange from around the world. Another alternative, now being investigated by the CME and Reuters, is to establish a 24-hour market through an automated electronic screen-based trading system.

There is, of course, the third possibility, one rarely mentioned in public by exchange officials. It could be that none of these exchange-based proposals will come to fruition. The 24-hour market in currency and stock derivatives could develop as an inter-bank market. Already, dealings in off-exchange currency hybrids surpasses the listed market. But exchange officials are usually quick to dismiss the purported benefits of bank customized currency contracts, arguing that such products are expensive compared to exchange-listed options and futures. For instance, a customized currency option will usually expire on the exact date that a corporate treasurer wants the foreign currency. That's not necessarily the most sensible strategy, however. An American-style option has both a time value and an intrinsic value. The intrinsic value is the amount to which an option is in-the-money, reflecting the value of the underlying instrument. The time value is the value of the option over and above its intrinsic value, and reflects the expectation of favourable movements in the underlying instrument. If an options position is closed out before the expiration date, the purchaser will gain to the extent that there is any time value attached to the option he holds. But if, as with customized options, the option is held until expiration, then there is no possibility of realizing a gain from the option's time value.

While exchange-listed products may make economic sense, treasurers often use customized products because they perceive their orders as too large to be handled on the exchange floor or because they want a tailor-made contract that reflects their financing needs. In the end, these arguments tend to be of little consequence in terms of the actual trading volume of the exchanges. Even if corporate treasurers turn to banks to get their future currency needs fulfilled, the banks in turn will often go to exchanges to lay off some of the risk they assumed.

CONCLUSION

So how are the world's currency and equity hybrid markets likely to develop? Stocks and stock derivatives are likely to be traded much more closely, if not actually on a side-by-side basis. For traders, the information advantages are enormous, particularly as they strive to avoid becoming victims of computerized trading programmes that exploit the slightest arbitrage opportunity. Even if regulatory organizations refuse to allow traders to deal in both stocks and stock derivatives at the same time, the markets are likely to see the development of faster and more efficient real time reporting of stock prices. Though side-by-side trading has advantages for dealers, it also opens the possibility of market manipulation. A trader may be tempted to manipulate stock prices in order to favour his long or short position in stock options and futures.

The future of trading links is still extremely difficult to predict. These links are only in their infancy, so harsh criticism might seem unjustified. Nonetheless, trading along these links has been disappointing, and it seems unlikely that innovations such as electronic order books will ever be that successful. Financiers are lovers of secrecy, and the preferred link is by way of telephone. More importance is attached to the development of identical contracts and improved international clearing. In an effort to claim uniqueness, some exchange officials have deliberately developed products that are different from those traded in other timezones. In future, hopefully the movement will be away from contrived uniqueness and towards fungible contracts. With fungible contracts, traders will quickly develop their own international trading links, and the liquidity of exchanges in different timezones will benefit as money is moved around the world from an exchange in one timezone to a different exchange in another timezone.

In the last 15 years, the emphasis has been on innovation in futures and options. The law of diminishing returns is now starting to take hold, however. It seems unlikely that a new innovation like the currency option or the stock index future will be introduced in the next few years. The reason is simple: all the permutations have been tried. Those still attracted by the orgy of innovations need merely look at the fate of the over-the-counter (OTC) stock index futures. When both the Chicago Mercantile Exchange and the Chicago Board of Trade introduced OTC futures contracts in October 1985, elaborate and expensive marketing campaigns were mounted and these instruments were touted as major new contracts. Both contracts flopped.

The exchanges that will be successful over the next few years will be those that emphasize improvements in existing instruments over the introduction of new products. If international clearing can be improved and identical products created, liquidity will increase and exchange-listed products will be more attractive to speculators and risk managers. That, more than anything, will help listed stock hybrids to prosper and allow the exchanges' currency contracts to successfully co-exist alongside the inter-bank market, thus ensuring that the exchanges continue to provide their important price discovery function.

Chapter 14

Issuing Abroad (1): The Black & Decker Corp.

Stephen F. Page

Throughout Black & Decker's 75-year history, many strategies have been necessary to provide financial support for the company's development. From the sale of S. Duncan Black's automobile for $600 to help fund the new company in 1910 through to the recent international equity offering, the financial management of Black & Decker has met many challenges. As with most corporations, Black & Decker had enjoyed general prosperity interspersed with short periods of financial difficulty. But from the beginning, when Black and Alonzo Decker founded the company, Black & Decker has consistently been innovative not only in its products, but also in its management. These two men captured the world power tool market with their development of the pistol grip and trigger switch, two innovations that are now standard on electric power tools. In 1964, the company once again demonstrated its engineering ability when it produced a cordless, minimum torque reaction space tool for use under weightless conditions by NASA's Apollo Lunar programme. The Lunar surface drill was used to remove samples from the moon. Today, this technology, which includes sophisticated battery recharging applications, has been carried forward in the development of a spectrum of labour saving cordless products marketed by Black & Decker. This innovative philosophy has helped the company to continue as a significant force within the power tool and small appliance industry, not only in the United States, but in the rest of the world as well.

As early as 1929, Black & Decker began manufacturing and selling products in England and Australia. Since then, the company has continued expanding its international presence to the point where it now has manufacturing facilities in 12 countries and markets its products in over 100 nations. But it is one thing to manufacture and sell throughout the world. It is quite another matter to have a recognized brand name in those markets. Because of Black & Decker's early entrance into the foreign market, its worldwide name recognition ranks with those of Coca Cola and IBM. Today, in the United Kingdom, name awareness of Black & Decker is over 90%. In Italy, Germany and France, it is over 80%. The name recognition is not only attributable to the many manufacturing locations in these countries over the years, but also to extensive consumer advertising of Black & Decker products. Worldwide publicity has been given to such labour-saving devices as electric drills, saws and sanders, electric garden equipment including lawn mowers, hedge trimmers, and weeders and, more recently, to household products such as dustbuster cordless vacuum cleaners, cordless mixers and knives, and the new automatic shut-off iron. Since the majority of Black & Decker products are used around the home, with Black & Decker having about a 50% share of almost all the markets it serves, it is understandable why the name recognition is so strong.

The 1960s and 1970s were years of prosperity for the company, with 15% per year sales and earnings growth. The early 1980s saw slower and less profitable expansion. Many factors contributed to this including the maturing of the consumer power tool markets and the growing competition from the Germans and the Japanese in the professional power tool market. This fierce competition had been aided by the strong dollar between 1980 and 1986. As a result, the company's sales had been flat since 1980, with the only increase coming from the 1984 acquisition of the General Electric small appliance division. This added $500 million to sales. (The acquisition price was $300 million, partly paid for through an issue of 3 million Black & Decker shares to General Electric.) The earnings difficulties were caused not only by the intense competition and a maturing marketplace, but also by significant productivity improvements that were achieved through the application of advanced technology in the manufacturing area. These advances included the substantial use of robotics which significantly increased unit volume at favourable costs. However, these productivity improvements require volume increases to have the appropriate payback. When volume doesn't increase, the product cost is affected by the lower factory utilization. During the early 1980s, Black & Decker was experiencing factory utilization of approximately 75%. With no significant increase in volume to absorb the added capacity, the factory utilization declined to 50–55%, causing a deterioration in the manufacturing margin.

The company responded in 1985 with a restructuring plan that was designed to increase the overall factory utilization from around 50% to about 75%. This was to be accomplished through the closure of two US and two French manufacturing locations and through the consolidation in both Italy and Germany of the company's manufacturing facilities into one plant location. The resulting $215 million restructuring charge was equal to 30% of Black & Decker's equity in 1985. The company ended its fiscal year, after the restructuring charge, with a debt to capital ratio of 42%. By contrast, the ratio had been 31% in 1984 and 24% in 1983. At the end of the fiscal year in September 1985, the company was confronted by more than just the restructuring charge of $215 million, which itself was greater than the earnings of the previous two years combined. In addition, the company suffered another sales decline from the previous year (if the General Electric small appliance acquisition is excluded) and net earnings (before restructuring) which were 50% of the 1984 level.

The company knew from the beginning that the restructuring plan would have a substantial cash cost. Unlike other restructuring plans where the majority of the charges are asset write-offs with very little cash cost, the Black & Decker restructuring included the closure of six plants and the transfer of the assets to other manufacturing locations, as well as the write-off of some excess equipment. The majority of the restructuring charge was the severance costs of over 3000 workers and the cost of moving machinery and equipment to other Black & Decker facilities. This would have added over $100 million in debt to a balance sheet that was already strained with a debt to capital ratio of 42%. This proposed increased leverage was also a concern to the company's rating agencies who had given the company's debt an 'A' rating. These ratings were clearly in jeopardy unless some action was taken to improve the balance sheet in the near term.

During 1985 the good news for Black & Decker was the strong stock market, with the Dow Jones Industrial Average increasing from 1184 in January to 1329 in September. The company's stock had stayed in a trading range of $17–$26 during 1985. Although the stock reacted to the write-off, it held in the low 20s during the latter part of 1985. The company reviewed various alternatives to improve its financial condition, but the company had no undervalued assets, no business segments which could be sold and there were no significant properties that could be sold and then leased back. The only alternative for improving the balance sheet was equity. But would the market take an equity issue at about $20 per share when the recent restructuring charge had taken the book value of the company from $13.50 to $10 per share? Could Black & Decker issue equity within a matter of weeks after the write-off of 30% of its equity?

This question was raised with one of the company's investment bankers. After due consideration, they responded in the affirmative. They felt that the market had been strong for several months, the current tone was good, and the outlook was relatively bullish. In fact, the investment bank was so positive that they could issue for Black & Decker that they offered to do a 'block deal'. At the time, a 'block deal' was a relatively new concept whereby an investment bank agrees to buy all the offered shares at a negotiated price without the need for, or use of, a syndicate – the more traditional underwriting approach. The company considered this offer but had reservations about a block trade as opposed to syndication. Traditional syndication has the benefit of rewarding those investment banks that have provided services for extended periods without the appropriate compensation. It also is a significant inducement to those in the syndicate to continue to provide these services. The benefit of the block trade, however, is that it can be less expensive for the issuer since the selling and distribution can be quickly arranged and costs are lower. The company considered the pros and cons of the block trade versus syndication and decided to utilize the block trade. Cost was not the only determining factor in reaching this decision. At this time, Black & Decker's investment banking relationships were in the state of flux, and no significant relationship issues were perceived. In retrospect, it is unlikely that Black & Decker would use a block trade again.

After the block trade decision was made, the next issue reviewed by the company was whether or not the European market should also be tapped. It was a bold question given the apparent difficulty that even a US offering would have because of the financial condition of the company. A Euro-issue would obviously complicate the offering and could slow it to the point where the strong market would be lost. On the other hand, Black & Decker was interested in moving a significant number of shares into Europe if at all possible. The company believed that a European equity owner has a somewhat different investment philosophy. A US investor operates with a 'trader' mentality, while a European shareholder operates with an 'investor' mentality. The European would not be as concerned with quarterly results as his US counterpart, but would be a longer-term investor, thus creating some additional stability for the Black & Decker stock. As a result of its only other experience in the Euro market, Black & Decker was optimistic about European participation. In 1982, a 100 million Deutschmark Eurobond offering was launched. Since it was the first time that Black & Decker had come to that market and because of its name recognition, the bond offering was very successful. The offering was 30% oversubscribed and indications were that a DM200 million offering could have been sold.

It was agreed that a dual-tranche equity issue would be launched, with a significant block offered in Europe. The European tranche, however, would not be on a 'block' basis, but rather would be sold through a syndicate. While the syndicate of six European banks was on the small size, it did include all of Black & Decker's significant relationships. Now that the launch strategy had been agreed upon, the next question was the number of shares that should or could be offered. The company was interested in an offering that would significantly restore the equity lost through the restructuring charge, but not so significant that the market could not absorb it. The company had 51 million shares outstanding. It was decided to issue 7 million shares, an addition of 15% to the outstanding equity. Although the offering size was relatively large compared to other deals during this time, it was further inflated by another 1.5 million shares from General Electric. On acquiring the GE small appliance division in 1984, Black & Decker gave General Electric 3 million shares of restricted stock. The restriction prevented GE from selling any stock without Black & Decker approval for a two-year period. These shares were acting as an overhang in the market and Black & Decker considered this an opportunity to halve the overhang. General Electric was invited to participate by selling one half of their holdings. These shares were ultimately included in the offering.

With the offering strategy and size now agreed, the preparation of the SEC filing was initiated. A Form S-3 Registration Statement under the Securities Act of 1933 was used, though with one major difference from a US-only offering. The registration statement contained *two* prospectuses; one to be used in connection with the US and Canadian offering and one to be used in the concurrent international offering. The two prospectuses were identical in all respects except for the front pages. The US prospectus included the number of shares to be sold in America by the US underwriter. The international prospectus included the number of shares to be sold in Europe and identified the European syndicate. The US prospectus contained information about the General Electric shares being offered, but the international prospectus made no reference to GE. The last major difference between the two prospectuses was that the international prospectus had two pages devoted to the US tax consequences for non-US holders of the equity. This section covered withholding taxes on dividends, back-up withholding upon failure to file certain information, and the tax consequences resulting from the disposition of the shares.

The Form S-3 was filed in early December 1986, less than a month after the release of the 1985 earnings, which included the restructuring charge and the net loss of $158 million for the year. With the strong stock market, it was hoped that the SEC would not do a full review of the filing, but approve it within its customary 48-hour period. The issue would then be sold before the Christmas holidays. Because of current market conditions, the underwriter recommended that European road shows would not be necessary and that only a minimal US road show might be required. (A 'road show' is when the senior management of a company meet with prospective investors. This usually involves two or more meetings in each of five or more cities in a couple of days.)

None of this was to be. Because of the company's 1985 results, the SEC decided that they would undertake a full review, which would take two to three weeks, not 48 hours. At best, SEC approval would be received just before Christmas and at worst Black & Decker would not be able to issue until 1986. Every effort was made to speed up the review process, but the SEC had more concerns than just the Black & Decker filing. It seems that the strong stock market had created a flood of filings that needed review and Black & Decker was just one of many.

Christmas came and went. Nothing was heard from the SEC until the first week of January. Their comments were minimal and easily resolved. Upon receiving the good news, the underwriter began to solicit orders. Because of the continued strength of the stock market, a road show – even a minimal US road show – was deemed unnecessary. The company's reasons for restructuring and the outlook for the business were well known in the investment community, as proven by the influx of orders for the stock.

Everything was going well. The SEC had their questions satisfactorily resolved. The US book was exceptionally strong and the European book was adequate. The company was almost ready to issue. The date was 8 January 1986, an eventful date for those that follow the stock market. On that day, the market fell 39 points, then the largest one-day loss in its history. The once solid book of orders for 8.5 million shares no longer existed. The underwriters and senior management regrouped and put together a new strategy. A US road show was now necessary and could be arranged in a few days. A European road show would be helpful, but at least two weeks were needed to make the necessary arrangements.

When the US road show began, the stock stood at $19, a 10% drop since the registration statement was filed in early December. It was decided that the European road show would be arranged if the book was not filling adequately after the first few days of the US road show. Senior management visited six cities in three days making multiple calls in each city. The story was well received and the book began to fill again. The Black & Decker stock price started to recover along with the rest of the stock market. With this renewed optimism, the underwriter decided the European road show was unnecessary. In retrospect, this was not a good decision. Given Black & Decker's European aim – selling to investors who would take a longer view of the company's performance – the Europeans should have had the same opportunity to meet with senior management and hear the turnaround story. Despite this mistake, the Euro-tranche of two million shares was sold, largely because of the Black & Decker name recognition. On 15 January 1986, the offering was sold in the US and Europe at a price of 20-1/8 per share, a recovery from its earlier low. Although the offering was unusual because of the 'block' US deal and a simultaneous Euro-tranche, the objectives were achieved. The issue significantly strengthened Black & Decker's balance sheet and placed an additional 2 million shares with European investors. Management's subsequent visits with these European investors has confirmed Black & Decker's earlier belief that they are 'investors' and not 'traders'.

Chapter 15

Issuing Abroad (2): Maxicare Health Plans Inc.

Fred W. Wasserman

As the leading managed health care company in the United States, Maxicare Health Plans, Inc. seeks the stability that can be achieved by having its stock widely held by investors who take a long-term view of the company. A wider distribution of ownership provides a more solid foundation for any company, especially if that company has charted a challenging growth course. It can help protect against the risk of sudden unjustified dumping of stock by institutional holders responding to a temporary dip in quarterly earnings. The company has also found that stockholders tend to think more as investors than as traders if they are given good reason to be loyal to the company. One of the most appropriate ways for any large publicly owned company to expand ownership of its stock is by deliberately allocating all or part of a new stock offering for overseas placement.

Maxicare made such an equity offering in 1985, allocating a minority proportion of shares for direct placement in Europe, with a majority offering occurring simultaneously in the United States and Canada. Some 10% of the company's stock is now held abroad, most of it in the United Kingdom. There are smaller holdings in France and Switzerland, primarily convertible bonds rather than stock. The decision to organize an offering in Europe, as well as the US, was the culmination of a trend the company had been observing. There had been growing interest from Europe in all of Maxicare's stock and convertible bond issues since the company went public in 1983. In addition to this obvious demand, the company found that many of the European institutions fit the ideal investor profile. They tended to be loyal and invest for the long run. Moreover, a significant number of European investors were keenly interested in the growth potential of the American health care industry. The company felt there would be a sympathetic hearing for a proven company that needed funding for well-planned strategic growth.

The company knew, then, that any new offering would attract European buyers. The unanswered question was: if Maxicare placed part of the offering in Europe, would the overseas holdings of the company's stock be extended more than if the company organized an offering in the United States and had the European buyers just tag along? Maxicare decided on the bilateral approach, and it was worth the effort. About a million shares were sold in Europe, probably twice as many as Maxicare could have sold had it issued just in the United States with only incidental selling to the European institutions. The November 1985 offering, with its bilateral approach, was something of a pioneering concept at the time. Maxicare registered six million shares with the Securities and Exchange Commission, allocating five million to the United States and one million to Europe. But, before saying anything more about the offering, one question needs to be answered: why did the company need the funds raised by the offering?

Maxicare owns and operates a system of health maintenance organizations (HMOs). Members who enrolled in these HMOs through their employer are provided with comprehensive health care services in return for a predetermined, prepaid monthly premium. These services are arranged by contracting on a prospective basis with physician groups for a fixed fee per member, per month, regardless of the extent and nature of services, and with hospitals and other providers under a variety of fee arrangements. The HMO industry has been expanding very rapidly in recent years, winning market share from the traditional group insurance companies who have been slower to adopt systems of managed health care. Because of the competitive dynamics within the HMO industry, Maxicare needed to expand and establish a presence in as many of the major markets in the United States as possible. The company needed to spearhead its development by marketing aggressively to Fortune 500 and other large employers. Increasingly, these employers prefer the option of a uniform national HMO service for all their plants and office locations in different cities and states. And Maxicare needed the economies of scale that national expansion would bring.

In 1985, the HMO industry was entering a consolidation phase. The number of HMO start-ups had mushroomed during the early 1980s and many of them did not have the management expertise or financial resources to continue flourishing independently. Given Maxicare's goal of national expansion, the company wanted to be positioned so that it could take advantage of the shake-out by purchasing rival HMO companies that were ripe for acquisition. Acquisitions were looked for in markets that made strategic sense in terms of Maxicare's expansion plans. And the companies sought were those whose lowered price reflected the difficulties they were experiencing in the marketplace. Maxicare needed a war chest so that it would have the funds at hand when the company was ready to make a move. Perceptive overseas investors following the American HMO industry already understood what the company was to emphasize during its European presentations: the eventual leaders in managed health care would be those strategically positioned to expand wisely through the consolidation phase. These investors bought the company's stock based on their understanding that Maxicare could use the funding as a springboard to national leadership in the HMO industry.

The lessons Maxicare learned in preparing for and launching its equity offering abroad could be useful for other companies considering such an approach. There were seven key elements to this process:

- *Your company's growth prospects*. It helps considerably to be perceived as a company on the move and/or well positioned in an industry that is attracting interest because of its potential to change the way people live or do business.
- *You must do your homework*. You must know your investors, their needs and preferences. Know their perceptions and misperceptions about your company. Then you can tailor your presentations to clarify any areas that are poorly understood. They will certainly do their homework about you. Europeans tend to be much more investigative than buy-side analysts in the United States. They will read all the analyst reports on your company and may bring them to meetings for reference.
- *Build credibility and dependability*. You need to make not one but several trips to explain your company before a major offering. This process enables investors to 'pace' the company for a period before their investment capital is at risk. They see objectives being met and learn more about key management figures. One trip just prior to your offering is not enough.
- *Demonstrated management excellence*. It is crucial that investors meet and get to know the most senior management figures. This is probably the single most important factor in convincing overseas investors that your company can do what it plans to do. They must have confidence that management has the necessary vision, energy and proven experience to do the job over the long run.
- *Convincing presentations*. You must be able to explain succinctly, persuasively and memorably just what your company's objectives are. This must be done in the manner and style with which overseas investors are comfortable, taking into account particular national and cultural characteristics.
- *After-sales service*. You need to make return trips periodically to your overseas investment centres just to reassure equity buyers that they made the right decision. Several of the major investing institutions will occasionally want to visit your company. Sufficient time should be allocated for them to meet with and be briefed by senior management.
- *Investment banking team*. You cannot operate without skilled support. The selection of a competent and experienced group of investment bankers is important. You may need to use a syndicate of banks, each with its own speciality niche, to expand your reach. Some banks will offer you additional contacts in selected regional financial centres, or offer broad experience in handling a particular type of investment product, such as convertible bonds.

So what perception did European institutional investors have of the HMO industry and Maxicare's place in it? European investors in general, but pre-dominantly the British, have always been interested in the United States as an area of growth and opportunity. They poured a lot of money into financing the expansion of America's frontier. In a sense, the American railroad companies were one of the premier growth stocks of the late nineteenth century. English and Scottish institutions were prominent among those funding America's westward development. To this day, they remain important players. While it is true that London remains pivotal as a financial centre – recycling funds not just from the UK but from all over the world – regional centres, such as Scotland's financial capital, Edinburgh, should not be neglected. Edinburgh has been a rich source of venture funding for start-ups and investment for growth companies. Institutions such as the Scottish Widows Trust are substantial buyers of equity. American hi-tech companies, like Apple Computer, quickly found favour there. Regional financial centres often concentrate on sifting for stocks whose potential is not yet widely known. They like to invest before the stock gets pounced on by the national and international brokerage houses.

Maxicare has been helped by the growing popularity of health care stocks over the last 10 years. The Europeans do not have publicly traded home-grown equivalents, so they fell in love with what was available in the United States. Some of the hospital management companies, for example, have done an excellent job in identifying this investment demand and benefiting from it. HMOs are seen as a well-managed private sector alternative to government health care organizations, particularly in the UK, where the National Health Service has been criticized for waste and bureaucratic inefficiencies. Indeed, privatization has become a rallying cry for investors in the UK under the Conservative government of Margaret Thatcher. Giant utilities, airlines and auto companies have been returned from public to private ownership with resulting excitement at the time of each new stock offering. In each field, the private sector is seen as being able to organize better and respond more effectively and rapidly to developments in the marketplace, shifts in the balance of demand and supply, and changes in consumer preferences. Indeed, Maxicare feels that there may well be future opportunities for the development of American-style HMOs in the UK.

What do investors see when they change their focus from the big picture of health care to Maxicare itself? They see a company that started as a small prepaid health plan in an obscure district of Los Angeles and became the largest investor-owned HMO company in the United States in less than 14 years. They see a depth of management, experience and expertise in what the company does. They know by observing the companies that have tried their hand at building HMOs that this business is no place for amateurs. But no matter how well they appear to think of your company, it is necessary for you to have a good knowledge of your potential investors. Maxicare has found it unwise to take it for granted that all aspects of the company's operation are understood. While investors may have a glowing overall opinion of your company's prospects, overseas investors may have misgivings about certain aspects of your plans, misgivings that may not have surfaced among US-based investors. The best way to ensure that you are prepared to address all the valid issues is to do your homework thoroughly. Read all the relevant overseas business publications and research reports.

Once you are well prepared, it is vital to take the time needed to build credibility among the targeted investment community by meeting with investors face to face. A series of canned presentations will not do. They really have to see the whites of your eyes. With this in mind, Maxicare has made several visits to Europe since going public just to meet with portfolio managers and others to explain the company. They were invited to come and question, test and evaluate. The company then made follow-up presentations and cultivated an interest in HMOs and the Maxicare approach. Some of these road shows were gruelling. They were usually week-long trips with a packed schedule of working breakfasts, lunches and dinners. One-on-one meetings took up any other available time. We needed to use a private jet to hop from meetings in Zurich, Paris and Geneva because scheduled airlines would not have left us enough time for meaningful contact with potential investors. But this intensive approach was necessary because in a short time span we met directly with all the principal investors.

First, the company built name recognition. Then, over time, potential investors got to know Maxicare in depth. A mutual understanding and trust was developed, on a personal as well as a professional level. Now institutional holders feel they know the company's senior management and they do not hesitate to phone to discuss how Maxicare's stock is performing. Thus, when the offering was made Maxicare was not suddenly appearing to tell the greatest story ever told. Many of them could remember the company from one, two, perhaps three years earlier. They could recall what was said in earlier meetings and see how much of it had been confirmed by subsequent market developments.

The meetings not only provided information for investors but allowed them to evaluate senior management as well. Confidence in management is crucial, probably the most important element in winning over potential investors. The key is to show that management is sound from the top and down through the ranks. Maxicare did not always send exactly the same management team. Sometimes investors had the opportunity to meet with the senior vice-president for marketing. On other occasions the company highlighted its financial experience and strength by including the chief financial officer. Investors were given a good feel for the range and depth of management expertise and how the different departments contribute to overall strength. For example, Maxicare's management information system (MIS) is regarded as one of the largest and most sophisticated in the HMO industry. The company regards it as the backbone of operations and an essential element in maintaining Maxicare's leadership position. It was important to explain in detail the scope of the company's MIS and illustrate how well management is equipped to process the staggering amount of varied daily data. This showed how effectively Maxicare has been using the latest technologies to serve the company's objectives.

When it comes to making presentations to overseas investors, you have to be flexible. Be sure to explain yourself very well. Be redundant if necessary. Use graphics – with hard copy booklets for distribution – to highlight the key messages. Maxicare's presentations were similar to those the company creates for analysts in the United States. As chairman and chief executive, I generally use a lot of graphics and slides to illustrate the key points. Then I talk around each slide to explain and elaborate. I don't give a prepared speech or a series of canned statements with each slide because this becomes too stilted. It is also repetitive and lacks punch for those who have seen earlier presentations. I speak conversationally and spend additional time explaining a particular concept if the audience appears to need more clarification. I can also tailor the examples and illustrations I give for each point so that it is meaningful for that audience, whether in London, Paris or New York.

If you are talking in terms that apply only to your business, you need to define those terms. For example, Maxicare had to explain the basic concept of HMOs in some cases. Even though most who attended the company's presentations had read extensively about Maxicare's activities in the United States, they were still unclear about details of how the company operates and how its system compared with systems they were used to in their own countries. Then there is the perception of the future, usually judged from the company's track record as well as its plans and strategies. Foreign investors are less stringent than Americans in demanding detailed five- or ten-year plans. These tend to lose meaning, anyway, the further into the future you project. Even though you are speaking the same language, you have to be aware of colloquialisms that do not easily translate. Be careful that Americanisms are understood.

After the offering, you have to provide comprehensive 'after-sales service' just as any reputable corporation does when it sells a product. You need to reassure the buyers that they made the right decision. You need to welcome representatives of the institutions when they want to pay you a visit. Show them around. Let them see that you are a real living and breathing organization. Show how the company intends to fulfil the expectations of investors over the long run. No matter how strong the fundamentals of a company and the prospects for its long-term growth are, it can suddenly come in for a ferocious mauling by the market. A couple of quarters of disappointing earnings and it no longer matters whether you are strategically sound. Your overseas investors will be much more inclined to hold your stock if you have taken time to keep them updated on the reasons why they should not pay heed to a temporary shift in market psychology.

The selection of an investment banking team is important in facilitating an equity issue. Maxicare's 1985 offering was handled domestically as a block trade by Salomon Brothers and Montgomery Securities. In Europe, it was syndicated by Salomon Brothers International Ltd in conjunction with seven other investment banks: Credit Commercial de France, Hill Samuel & Co. Ltd, Morgan Grenfell & Co. Ltd, Credit Suisse First Boston Ltd, Montgomery Securities, Swiss Bank Corporation International Ltd and Union Bank of Switzerland (Securities) Ltd. Salomon Brothers worked with these financial partners in order to draw on their specialized knowledge of those different countries where an appetite for new health care stock had been identified. All the participating investment banks had expertise in certain market niches as well as in the targeted countries.

So which companies should consider the possibility of an overseas equity offering? The company should be a good-sized player in the marketplace, with a lot of actively traded shares outstanding. The stock of blue-chip companies is sought for its reputed solidity, safety and stability. But there is increasing interest in stocks with growth potential, especially if the company is viewed as being in the early stages of a fast-growth cycle. Overseas investors want to cash in on the entrepreneurial vitality of American business. A superior growth vehicle with a solid balance sheet provides the most exciting opportunity, whether the product involved is hi-tech or tennis shoes, or a new way to organize an old activity. Unlike the United States, there are fewer start-up companies and growth-stock possibilities in Europe. Ideally, investors like to spot companies that are setting trends or profiting directly from them. They seek companies in businesses that are changing the way people live their lives or do business. And, like all investors, they prefer to find them before their price/earnings ratios and other indicators have become stratospheric. Any company that needs additional funding and meets these criteria should at least consider the possibility of an overseas equity offering.

Chapter 16

Editor's Conclusion: Risk, Regulation and Politics

The global equity market is likely to become a riskier venture for all concerned, bankers, corporations and investors. The market was one of the chief beneficiaries of the bull market. The run up in stock prices from August 1982 to October 1987 made it easier to place equity internationally, turning this market into one of the fastest growing segments of the international capital markets. Over the past few years, investors have, as never before, looked abroad for undervalued stocks to form part of their diversified portfolios. Internationally traded equities, taking their lead from buoyant domestic markets, have attracted considerable investor interest. But with the bull market now over, a new, harsher phase in the development of the international stock market has emerged. It is unlikely, however, that a bear market will kill the process of internationalization. There is no reason why a turndown in the market should make investors any less interested in foreign stocks.

Even if global trading is badly hit, reflecting the importance of domestic stock markets in setting the pace for most internationally traded shares, the primary placement market is unlikely to die. The commitment to an international equity market by the major investment banks, and the equity syndication skills developed over the last few years, should ensure the market's continued development. Moreover, the internationalization of equity has increased the transaction-oriented nature of the market and thus provided banks and brokers with a host of additional fees: for stock custody when issuing depositary receipts, for the currency conversion of dividends, for swapping the bond portion of a bond plus warrant issue. Following the market downturn, however, the prevalent form of new equity issue is likely to change, with even greater use made of bonds with warrants and convertible bonds.

Nonetheless, a bear market means greater risks for the investment banks involved in new equity or equity-related issues. As competition for business grows more intense, and underwriting and management fees tighten, the syndication expertise of banks will be tested to the full. Using bond salesmen to sell equity and sending potential investors paltry research material will no longer suffice. If the bought deal techniques of Canada and the United States also become common for international straight equity issues, then the risks will be even greater. While the international use of these techniques benefits both corporations and bankers by allowing them to seize market opportunities quickly, it also increases the risk that they may fail to provide potential investors with accurate material information.

Moreover, risks are being increased by the search for deregulated markets, where the competition is more intense and investors less protected. All else being equal, market participants will tend to use the least regulated market for issuing new equity and trading existing shares. Corporations benefit from lower issuing costs, with the necessary disclosure, registration and legal costs less burdensome. Investment bankers are forced to compete more keenly for business, but the higher trading and issuing volume tends to compensate for the reduced fees they receive on a deal-by-deal basis. Keener competition, tighter trading spreads and lower, negotiated commissions also benefit investors, though investors should be aware of both the additional fees they may have to pay for the likes of dividend currency conversion and stock custody and also the exchange rate risk incurred when investing in a foreign equity.

Up until now, all markets have patently not been equal, as the continued growth of the heavily regulated US equity market makes clear. The American market may suffer from a glut of regulation, but it also enjoys a glut of liquidity. While the grip of US exchanges on the trading volume in US stocks is not under threat, America's exchanges (with the exception of NASDAQ) have not fared well when attracting foreign listings or trading volume in foreign stocks. There are signs that even the once all-dominant New York Stock Exchange is worried about the threat from abroad. In March 1987, officials at the exchange sought to ban Big Board members from trading on the London Stock Exchange during those hours when the New York Stock Exchange is open. The proposed ban would have extended to some 200 stocks that are listed on both exchanges. Big Board officials justified the ban by arguing that the London Stock Exchange no longer constituted an exchange following its decision to abandon floor trading and move over to an electronic system of NASDAQ-style competing market makers.

The New York Stock Exchange subsequently reversed its decision, but the feeling has persisted that this was the hasty decision of an endangered species. Following London's deregulation in 1986, there is now a significant regulatory imbalance between London and its two rival financial centres, Tokyo and New York. Japan's capital market continues to benefit from the country's growth, the increasing recognition of the yen and the high savings rate. The US capital markets enjoy no such benefits. Early indications showed that post-Big Bang London was doing 50% more business in foreign stocks than the various American markets combined, reflecting the increased competition in London's deregulated and newly-adopted electronic marketplace. The emergence of the

Euro-equity market is partly a reflection of the burdensome regulations of the US markets, just as the Eurobond market's growth was in response to the 1963 imposition of the interest equalisation tax by the United States. If London, and the European equity market generally, continue their renaissance, the US market may appear increasingly unattractive for foreign companies seeking a foreign listing or wanting to raise equity abroad. As a corporation, why suffer the registration and disclosure problems of a US stock issue if the shares can be sold elsewhere with greater ease? Even US issuers are starting to look abroad in great numbers. American companies like Borland International, Mrs Fields, International Signal and Control and Dataserv have eschewed the US market and gone public in London. Not only are issuing costs lower, but also European shareholders – unlike their American counterparts – tend to have the mentality of the stock investor rather than the stock trader.

It's not just American companies that are looking to the European market. Long frustrated by the Glass-Steagall Act and its restriction on their investment banking activity, US commercial banks like Bankers Trust and Chase Manhattan have considered abandoning their bank charters. Already they are expanding in London beyond Washington's regulatory grasp. American banks are well-established participants in the Eurobond market, underwriting and selling debt instruments, doing abroad what they cannot do at home. The next step, the trading, underwriting and selling of equity by US commercial banks, has already begun. In 1986, for instance, Citicorp helped underwrite international equity issues for Newscorp Finance and Nuovo Pignone, while Bankers Trust was a co-manager in the Feldmuhle Nobel deal. The Federal Reserve allows commercial banks operating abroad to take positions in stocks, but this is limited to $2 million for any one company's equity. Hoare Govett, now 83% owned by Security Pacific, raised the limit on its underwriting exposure from $2 million to an unspecified figure over $150 million through the simple expedient of using a sub-underwriting group. These US commercial banks are undertaking risks that the legislators who drafted Glass-Steagall would have considered unacceptable.

But what about 24-hour trading? Surely the US market is an integral part of the continuous marketplace based on three timezones each trading for eight hours each? Surely not. America's bank regulators interpret the Glass-Steagall Act as having no extra territorial application. So why don't US commercial banks set up a single dealing room in London or Tokyo and trade round the clock from there, gathering in orders from around the world? A leap of fantasy? In 1986, Washington's regulators ruled that the London stockbroker Vickers da Costa could continue as a NASDAQ market maker for foreign securities even after Citicorp purchased the firm, as long as Vickers New York only acts as an agent in any transaction. All the market making risk is assumed by Vickers in London. There is no reason why the precedent set by this decision should not be extended so that commercial banks can deal in internationally traded US securities in the same manner.

Despite this possibility, the choice for US policy makers is not so simple. Scrapping Glass-Steagall and removing the onerous securities registration and corporate disclosure requirements would have costs as well as benefits. Allowing commercial banks to act as investment banks would call forth memories of the banking débâcle following the 1929 crash. It would not, however, seem an impossible task to allow commercial banks into investment banking activity while at the same time imposing safeguards to reduce the risks to bank depositors. When compared to the rewards, the risks of investment banking are, arguably, no less great than those undertaken in the past by commercial banks when lending to the Third World or dabbling in off-balance-sheet liabilities. With Japanese commercial banks now needing to recycle the massive surpluses generated by the Japanese economy, heightening the possibility that the banks will end up lending to uncreditworthy borrowers, this issue is likely to become even more pressing in Japan.

While scrapping Glass-Steagall seems far from dangerous, removing the onerous disclosure and registration requirements would strip away the much-valued protection of shareholders. The Securities and Exchange Commission has made some concessions to foreign issuers and is now considering further efforts to facilitate US securities issues by foreign corporations. Nonetheless, Washington's politicians and regulators are unlikely to reduce radically the level of investor protection, particularly in the wake of the ongoing insider trading scandal. Though the issues raised by the scandal are not logically related to the question of shareholder protection from misleading corporate financial information, nonetheless the two issues are tougher to separate in practice. Even without these current concerns, it is not easy to strike a balance between, on the one hand, the need for shareholder protection and, on the other hand, the demand by corporations for easier access to new equity capital. Though finding this balance is a political issue, the economic consequences cannot be ignored.

*   *   *

The distribution of share ownership, like the question of shareholder protection, is a political as well as an economic issue. In the past, political and social commentators have offered numerous theories about the impact of the distribution of share ownership. Privatization has been touted as a way of establishing a shareholders' democracy. The massive investments by union pension funds were going to give us a workers' democracy. The trend towards giving employees an equity interest in companies will, some argue, give us an industrial democracy. So what will the internationalization of share ownership give us?

Manchester liberals argued that free trade would so entwine the world that war and its disruption of international commerce would be disavowed. But those dreams drowned in the quagmire of the Great War's trench battles. Only the most naïve would now make the same claims for the internationalization of share ownership as the Manchester liberals made for the internationalization of commerce. Indeed, those involved in the international equity market are more likely to be on the defensive against the rantings of the petty nationalists. When money is pouring out of the country and into foreign stocks, the petty nationalists cry aloud about the draining away of the nation's resources. And when the money is pouring into the country as foreigners grab a stake in our companies, the petty nationalists tell us that foreigners are stealing our industries and sucking away our profits. But contradictory statements aside, there are real issues of corporate accountability and responsibility. Will XYZ Corporation's foreign shareholders do anything (other than sell out) if XYZ stagnates, with costs rising and innovations failing to materialize? Will they care if the corporation pollutes the waters and sacks the workers? Indeed, will these investors turn up at the annual general meeting or even bother to return their proxy voting forms?

Few governments have made any sort of a decision on these issues (and, when they do, it normally adds to the burden of regulation and thus spurs the growth of other, less regulated markets). Some governments limit foreign share ownership of domestic companies. Others have imposed exchange controls, though usually in response to short-term currency crises. Privatizations have involved the selling of stock abroad, but this is usually done because the stock issue is perceived as too large for the domestic market (though the international ownership that results undoubtedly makes it more difficult for any future government to re-nationalize the company).

To date, the international equity market has been driven by a combination of forces largely unconcerned with the national interest. Investors now want a diversified portfolio. Corporate treasurers see greater stability in an international shareholder base. Investment bankers have been anxious intermediaries, glad of the chance to make money while sharpening international syndication skills. Beyond the most basic of political grunts, the politicians have largely ignored the question of whether the global equity market will threaten corporate accountability and national stability. Once again, the international capital markets have run ahead of the national political grasp.

Index